SEEING THE WORLD
WITH ABORIGINAL EYES

A Four Directional Perspective on
Human and non-Human Values, Cultures and
Relationships on Turtle Island

Brian Rice

SEEING THE WORLD
WITH ABORIGINAL EYES

A Four Directional Perspective on
Human and non-Human Values, Cultures and
Relationships on Turtle Island

Written by Brian Rice

Edited by Jill Oakes and Rick Riewe
Produced by
Department of Zoology,
Department of Environment and Geography, and
Clayton H. Riddell Faculty of Environment, Earth, and
Resources
University of Manitoba

Winnipeg

Aboriginal Issues Press

2005

iv

Seeing the World with Aboriginal Eyes, A Four Directional Perspective on Human and non-Human Values, Cultures and Relationships on Turtle Island is a refereed publication. Information and perspectives presented in this book are the sole opinions of the author and not those of the University of Manitoba or the Aboriginal Issues Press, its employees, editors, and volunteers. All profits from the sale of this book are used to support the refereed publication of Aboriginal scholarship and the Aboriginal Issues Press Scholarship endowment fund at the University of Manitoba.

© 2005 Aboriginal Issues Press
        Clayton H. Riddell Faculty of Environment, Earth, and Resources
        University of Manitoba
        Winnipeg, Manitoba, R3T 2N2

Phone (204) 474-7352   Fax (204) 474-7699
E-Mail   aboriginal-issues-press@umanitoba.ca

Other publications available from Aboriginal Issues Press:
        Aboriginal Health, Identity and Resources
        Pushing the Margins: Native and Northern Studies
        Working with Aboriginal Elders
        Native Voices in Research
        Aboriginal Cultural Landscapes
        Gambling and Problem Gamblng in First Nations Communities

For information on the following pre-1999 publications, please contact Ms. Elaine Maloney at the Canadian Circumpolar Institute (780) 492-4512:
        Human Ecology: Issues in the North, Volumes I, II, and III
        Issues in the North, Volumes I, II, and III

Cover Design by Karen Armstrong Design; Printing by Hignell Printing Ltd., Winnipeg

Canadian Cataloguing in Publication Data

Rice, Brian, 1955-
Seeing the world with Aboriginal eyes : a four directional
perspective on human and non-human values, cultures and relationships on Turtle Island
/ written by Brian Rice ; edited by Jill Oakes and Rick Riewe.

Includes bibliographical references.
ISBN 0-9686138-6-1

1. Indians of North America--Religion. 2. Ethnoscience--Canada. 3. Ethnoscience--United States. I. Oakes, Jill E. (Jill Elizabeth), 1952- II. Riewe, R. R. (Roderick R.) III. Title.

E98.R3R52 2005   299.7   C2005-900935-7

This book is dedicated to

The Late Jake Thomas, Kaokwa:haka Elder

and

The Late Art Solomon, Anishnawbe Elder.

TABLE OF CONTENTS

Acknowledgements

From a time when I worked at the University of Sudbury, Department of Native Studies, I thank Alice Dickson who edited *Seeing With A Native Eye,* Mary Recollet, the best Administrative Assistant in any department, and Kenneth-Roy Bonin, President, without whose permission, this book would not have been written. I thank Jill Oakes and Rick Riewe for the final editing and publishing of the book.

I acknowledge all of the students in the Traditional Knowledge and Recovery of Indigenous Mind doctoral programs, formally at the California Institute of Integral Studies. Particularly Pamela Colorado, the Director of both programs, who allowed me the chance to learn from many Indigenous elders during our residencies in California, Mexico, Senegal, Hawaii, Lappland and Arizona and made it possible to learn more about my own Mohawk traditions in Rotinonshonni territory now called Central New York. I acknowledge some of the traditional teachers and elders from that program such as Gwendalle Cooper - Cherokee, Masalt Golindo - Aztec, Humbatzmen - Mayan, Ralph Amouq - Inupiaq, Lyons Kapiyo'ho - Hawaiian, Hale Makua - Hawaiian, Ester Pinosa - Miwok, and others who if not included in this book certainly influenced its making.

I also thank Anishnawbe traditionalist Jim Dumont, for his contribution to this manual, whose format came from his teachings. I also gratefully acknowledge and thank Anne Solomon for reviewing the section on her father, Elder Arthur Solomon; and Yvonne Thomas, who made it possible for myself and others to learn about the Rotinonshonni traditions from her late husband Chief Jacob Thomas, both a friend and teacher and who was a living embodiment of traditional knowledge. And of course I am sincerely grateful and thank the late Anishnawbe elder Arthur Solomon, who for many of us, was an example on how we should conduct our lives for the betterment of Aboriginal People.

Foreword

Seeing the World with Aboriginal Eyes evolved from a manual I wrote while teaching in the Department of Native Studies, University of Sudbury, and while continuing my doctoral studies in the Aboriginal Traditional Knowledge Program, California Institute of Integral Studies. It is influenced by my experiences with elders who taught in that program, including Humbatzmen (Mayan) , Mazalt Golindo (Aztec), Ralph "Grey Wolf" (Inupiaq), Art Solomon (Anishnawbe, co –founder of the University of Sudbury Native Studies Department) and Jacob Thomas (Cayuga, a hereditary chief of the Iroquois Confederacy).

The lack of material on Aboriginal spirituality and world view became apparent while teaching in the Department of Religious Studies, University of Winnipeg. Therefore, upon permission of Kenneth-Roy Bonin, President of the University of Sudbury, I immediately began expanding and converting my manual into a book.

Although world view is addressed by some Aboriginal authors, they primarily discuss the sacred circle and relationships within the circle; I refer to them as circle teachings. Based on a tradition of some non-Aboriginal academics misrepresenting or not acknowledging elders' teachings, Aboriginal authors are reluctant to delve deeply into Aboriginal spiritual knowledge for fear of being exploited. There is some truth to these concerns. However, based on my experiences as an Aboriginal academic involved in ceremonial life, and on others who are more knowledgeable than myself, there is no truth to the fear of giving away the secrets of sacred knowledge by writing them down. Most written literature provides only some basic fundamentals of sacred knowledge; I have never learned a sacred ceremony or song by reading a book. One understands Aboriginal spiritual knowledge only through years of practice and experience, not by reading a book. Also, years of training in sacred knowledge cannot be replicated by simply writing about the experience, for example, an author cannot replicate a nine-day oral recital of the Great Law of Peace in a brief chapter of ten pages. Therefore our fears of exploitation must not prevent us from writing about Aboriginal spiritual or cultural knowledge. It cannot be exploited only misrepresented.

I wrote this book for beginners interested in Aboriginal spirituality and world view, and it is especially suitable for students in programs such as: Native Studies, Religious Studies, Environmental

Studies, Peace Studies, or Aboriginal Philosophy. In the book I use the term 'they' when writing about Aboriginal people collectively and the terms 'our', 'us' and 'we' when being more specific, and when writing about the Rotinonshonni culture of which I am a part.

I examine the traditional sources of Aboriginal world views and spiritual understandings in terms of origins, relationships, nature of existence, self-knowledge and traditional teachings. Universal themes, patterns of manifestation, growth and change, perception of reality and levels of meaning are examined and explored through various Aboriginal cultures of North America. I derive meaning from traditional knowledge by studying the teachings of the past as a basis for alternative direction for contemporary society. This is done knowing that some contemporary Aboriginal peoples face difficulties retaining their traditional knowledge. I include Aboriginal knowledge from various traditions in North America, focusing on traditional knowledge from the Central and North Eastern regions of Canada and the United States, with an emphasis on teachings from southern Ontario.

The model used to shape this book was provided by Jim Dumont (1997), an Anishnawbe traditional teacher in the *Midewiwin* Lodge, following his description of the four basic teachings of the four directions encompassing the sacred circle of life (see front cover). The first section of the book corresponds with the Eastern Door, "The Seeing Path", including cosmology, vision, beliefs and values evolving from the spirit world. The second section of the book corresponds with the Southern Door, "Ways of Relating", including environment, interactions between Aboriginal people and other beings, the cycles of life, time, mathematics and numbers. The third section of the book corresponds with the Western Door, "Coming to Knowing", which includes elders, the learning path, and Aboriginal knowledge. Finally, the fourth section of the book corresponds with the Northern Door, "Ways of Doing", including ceremonies, healing, prayer and life ways. Each of these directions relate to personal fulfillment when people integrate an Aboriginal world view into their lives, including the sharing of knowledge, dreams, and states of being.

Other insights include an appreciation for and awareness of: traditional sources of Aboriginal world views and spiritual understandings; paths that Aboriginal people take in their search for truths in Aboriginal teachings; universal truths found within North American Aboriginal cultures; traditional teachings that influence the meaning of contemporary society's life and provide new directions; and commonalities in ways of knowing shared by diverse Aboriginal cultures.

This book provides an Aboriginal viewpoint, built primarily on Aboriginal authors; some good source material from non – Aboriginal authors is also included to elaborate on themes. These authors have sometimes inaccurately interpreted the material; those of us who have valid Aboriginal experiences and knowledge are better able to do this. Since beginning this manuscript eight years ago, there is significantly more primary source material from Aboriginal scholars. Today, Canadian Aboriginal scholars are in the forefront writing about Aboriginal knowledge and setting the boundaries. I hope *Seeing the World with Aboriginal Eyes* provides insights on the complexity of Aboriginal ways of knowing, contributes to the growing academic discourse, and inspires more Aboriginal scholars to continue researching and writing on this important topic.

Dr. Brian Rice
January 2005

Chapter One

EASTERN DOOR:
THE SEEING PATH--THE WORLD OF THE
SPIRIT

This section presents what *Seeing the World with Aboriginal Eyes* fully entails and critically explores some Aboriginal peoples' traditional understandings of the cosmos. There are different ways to look at the world, of interpreting phenomena, and situating oneself in the world. Aboriginal peoples have unique perspectives on their lives and their place in the cosmos. This section presents cosmos-related terminology, explores the challenges in interpreting and understanding Aboriginal perspectives, and examines the unique patterns of thinking and identifying Aboriginal world views.

The Complexity of *Seeing the World with Aboriginal Eyes*

What does *Seeing the World with Aboriginal Eyes* actually mean? How is it connected to belief systems and cosmologies of people? In order to understand the concept of *Seeing the World with Aboriginal Eyes*, we must first acknowledge that cultural groups interpret and explain natural phenomena, relationships and all the things in their existence in ways that are unique to their own cultural understandings. To answer these questions, we must first understand that Aboriginal peoples view the world around them in culturally distinct ways.

How can we learn what is unique and particular about Aboriginal peoples' understandings? Readings can be utilized as reference points, however, to fully *Seeing the World with Aboriginal Eyes*, means becoming immersed in a particular Aboriginal world view, being wholly integrated into a way of life, ceremonies, language and culture.

Can an outsider who lives within an Aboriginal society become immersed enough in the culture to truly understand its world view? This issue often arises with intermarriage and long-term residency and is pertinent to my experience as a person of both Mohawk and Finnish descent. It is a question I have asked myself many times. I have come to realize that even being born into a particular culture doesn't mean one is necessarily immersed in the traditions of that culture. Can a bi-cultural person function equally in both cultures, even if those cultures are at variance with each other, such as someone with both Aboriginal and non- Aboriginal ancestry? I believe so, however, a bi-cultural person will most likely be brought up with one predominant culture. The Métis, a symbiosis of both Aboriginal and European cultures, is a distinct culture. Often the European culture is dominant even when self-identification as an Aboriginal person, remains strong. Social engineering among Aboriginal people, created by the education system and government policies, has fragmented Aboriginal cultures, including Metis, from following fully integrated communal holistic ways of living to individualistic fractured ones. A case in point is, although I have been involved in Aboriginal traditional practices for many years, I am still reconstructing an identity based on lost Mohawk traditions. I have many years ahead of me before I achieve my goal of *Seeing the World with Aboriginal Eyes.* In contrast, I am continually exposed to my Euro-Canadian heritage, which is as difficult to lose as is the process of finding my Mohawk heritage.

Can a person educated in Euro-western language and thought completely let go of the cultural understandings formed when he/she was young? If so, can non-Aboriginal people who come to live or intermarry into Aboriginal societies truly understand that society? To adequately answer this, a few case histories are analyzed. A non-Aboriginal woman, Mary Jemison (1742-1833), lived with the Seneca for 64 years, mothered several Seneca children, and integrated into Seneca society when traditions were vibrant and strong (Seaver 1990). In her writings, Ms. Jemison tried to understand some aspects of Seneca culture which were alien to her original culture. Today, descendants of her offspring make up one of the most influential families in contemporary Seneca society. It appears that people can intimately understand another culture; however, they may never let go of the cultural concepts formed in childhood.

Another example of cultural immersion is the increased participation of non-Aboriginal peoples in Aboriginal ceremonies. Some Aboriginal elders openly teach individuals from any cultural affiliation. Also, culturally distinct traditions such as the yearly recitation of The Great Law at Six Nations, are now attended by both Aboriginal and non-Aboriginal people from outside the community. Does this provide these individuals from other cultures insight into the cultural nuances inherent in the Great Law? Hereditary Chief Jacob Thomas believed it was possible, with limitations, as even Aboriginal peoples raised without their original language struggle to understand; however, Thomas encouraged individuals to keep learning and eventually they would grasp most of the cultural intricacies.

Can an Aboriginal person raised away from his/her Aboriginal nation become fully integrated into that Aboriginal community as an adult? In the past, this was a common experience for students attending residential schools; it continues today as many Aboriginal people are raised in non-Aboriginal communities. Many of these individuals are also trying to integrate the non-Aboriginal understandings learned during their formative years with newly acquired Aboriginal cultural information. Some people acquire a mentor, cultural teacher, or an elder to help them on their journey, which is still a long, slow and laborious process.

Neither does growing up in an Aboriginal community ensure that an Aboriginal person becomes a cultural expert. Many Aboriginal peoples, including some leading scholars teaching in Native Studies programs, who were raised in their traditional community, neither speak their original language nor practice their traditions and ceremonies. These individuals also face the challenges of integrating Aboriginal concepts into their contemporary beliefs and thoughts. Unlike individuals raised in non-Aboriginal communities, people raised in their original community can access local elders; however, in communities with a strong Christian influence, elders are reluctant to teach their traditions. This reluctance is the legacy of colonialism, as well as the fact that elders raised in a fully integrated holistic way of life based on subsistence have difficulty practicing spiritual beliefs without the accompanying lifestyle. New expressions of Aboriginal spiritual practices have now evolved, adapting traditions into present day realities. Also, the recent migration of Aboriginal people to urban centres has provided urban Aboriginal youth with access to more traditional elders than they might have while living in their original communities.

Alternative Ways of Understanding

The process of *Seeing the World with Aboriginal Eyes* is a recognized phenomena; Aboriginal cultures possess ways of viewing the world that are unique from mainstream culture. There are common threads shared by all Aboriginal peoples, which have culturally distinct ways of being expressed by each Aboriginal culture.

This section explores Aboriginal and non-Aboriginal authors' perspectives on *Seeing the World with Aboriginal Eyes*. Toelken (1976) notes that Aboriginal people who have been brought up in their culture and later placed within the mainstream culture, experience many difficulties in adjustment. In spite of years of training in the residential school system, Aboriginal children could not fully integrate into mainstream culture. Often these children felt they belonged in neither culture and were confused about their place and role in society. Mi'kmag educator and scholar Mary Battiste, explains the impact that residential schools had on the psyche of Aboriginal youth and states "This educational process is called cognitive imperialism, the last stage of imperialism wherein the imperialist seeks to whitewash the tribal mind and soul to create doubt" (Barman *et al*.1989).

According to a non- Aboriginal author (Brown 1982), Aboriginal traditions are primal (not primitive) traditions evolving from the very beginnings of each specific society. Over the years, a key to the survival of these traditions is the ability to adapt, to be dynamic rather than static. For example, after the subsistence lifestyle ended, traditional Rotinonshonni (Iroquois) elders continued the cycle of ceremonies through the longhouse tradition, preventing these timeless cultural traditions from disappearing as has happened in some other Aboriginal societies and enabling the Rotinonshonni culture to survive and flourish. Even with severe culture loss, the core understandings and values held by each Aboriginal nation are retained by adapting to social changes, as seen in the Longhouse tradition of the Rotinonshonni and the *Midewiwin* Lodge tradition of the Anishnawbe. Traditional fundamental beliefs and patterns of thinking have remained for those individuals adhering to their teachings, regardless of social change.

Patterns of Thought: Circle

Patterns of thought set out by a culture help define that culture. For many Aboriginal peoples, a circle represents the space in which we live. This is reflected in our dances, ceremonies, and cosmologies. On the other hand, Toelken (1976) states that western society represent their space with straight lines, as seen in community plans, style of homes, and artwork. Circular patterns established by Aboriginal peoples help define us just as linear structures in western societies define those peoples.

Monotheism and Polytheism

To truly understand another culture, one must understand the language patterns, spirituality, knowledge systems and lifestyles. Otherwise one's own cultural reference points are used resulting in misconceptions. This is seen in ethnocentric writings by explorers, clergy, anthropologists and historians who have not been engaged in ethno-historical analysis and failed to interpret their experiences through the eyes of Aboriginal peoples. Is this possible to the extent necessary to understand another culture? A few anthropologists attempting to understand equated Aboriginal belief systems with belief systems that their own ancestors held. For instance, Aboriginal spiritual understandings are often viewed as "primitive" and polytheistic as opposed to contemporary religions, such as Christianity, which is viewed as being evolved and monotheistic. These cross-cultural judgments are biased, hierarchical, and pejorative to Aboriginal peoples, lacking cultural sensitivity and understanding.

Spiritual beliefs are often central to understanding world views. Brown (1982) believes Aboriginal spiritual beliefs lie in the middle between monotheism and polytheism, have nothing to do with the stages of evolution, and that what is referred to by Aboriginal peoples as the Great Mystery includes a wider spectrum of beliefs including energy fields and spirit worlds. Mayan elder Humbatzmen (1990) agrees, investigating energy fields and spirit worlds in his writings. He states that the Mayan word for the Creator, *Hunab K'u*, translates as movement and measure. *Hunab K'u* energy encompasses Mayan cosmology where the universe is both macrocosm and microcosm. Sa'ke'j Henderson (1992), a Choctaw who lived with the Mi'kmaq, has investigated energy fields and spirit worlds in his works. He states that among Algonquin peoples, such as the Mi'kmaq, Cree and Anishnawbe, the Great Mystery is referred to as *Kitchi Manitou* [Mantouk plural form]. Lesser beings inhabiting the spiritual realms are referred to as *Manitou,* their universe is both macrocosm and microcosm, with everything linked and in continual motion. That no separation exists between the two is fundamental to understanding Aboriginal peoples' cosmologies, including the world of spirits and nature. Although it was integral to early non-Aboriginal spiritual beliefs, Brown (1982) believes modern religions have forgotten that everything is interconnected and interrelated. This leads to western peoples' viewing nature as subdued while Aboriginal peoples see nature as living with each component integral to the other and with animals viewed as persons and not considered inferior to humans. Traditional Aboriginal ways of life are based on reciprocation with the rest of creation rather than the western way based on domination.

Although numerous Euro-American scholars reflected ethnocentricity in their writings, a few subdued their cultural biases and some were even transformed by their cross-cultural experiences, even though they avoided admitting this for fear of being ridiculed by colleagues. Irving Hallowell (1967) lived with the Anishnawbe of Northern Ontario and Manitoba. Privately he stated how he was profoundly affected by spiritual leaders in the Berens and Popular River.

His writing conformed to the standards set by the scientific institutions of the day. He appeared as a dispassionate observer, rarely commenting on anything beyond the explanation of scientific methods lest he be viewed as a fool. How could he not be? A person could be completely transformed by participating in Shaking Tent or Dark Room Ceremonies. While participating in the Journey of the *Peacemaker* excursions with Jacob Thomas and his wife Yvonne, I witnessed many Aboriginal and non-Aboriginal people having life transforming experiences. Another time, I witnessed a cold pot of water boil while someone held the pot in their hands, which helped me question preconceived notions about world views and increased my respect for Aboriginal traditions and belief systems. Duncan Campbell Scott, Department of Indian Affairs, wrote *Powason's Drum*, (Cleaver 1974) based on his encounter with a medicine man seen as evil by his Christian belief system. Hallowell and Scott's cultural ways of understanding failed to support their search for meaning in their cross-cultural experiences. It is their loss. Others have been much more fortunate.

Hallowell (1967), did gain some insight into Anishnawbe life without imposing his own cultural values, including Aboriginal ways of knowing time and space. He recognized Anishnawbe viewed dream sequences as real events that transcended temporal and non-temporal time and space and that Anishnawbe believed in *memengweciwak (Little People)* who lived in both the temporal and spiritual world. Hallowell (1967) recorded the importance of including all aspects of each experience based on that person's world view, including experiences incomprehensible to non-Aboriginal researchers.

Non- Aboriginal views of Aboriginal cultures have changed from understanding cultures through the cultural biases of the viewer to attempting to understand cultures from Aboriginal peoples' perspectives, and to the rise of the Aboriginal elder guru. In the 1970's, the Aboriginal elder guru as holder of Aboriginal wisdom evolved from the popularization of the Mahara-ji of India by the Beatles (Barreiro 1992). Edward Benton-Banai, an elder of the *Midewiwin* lodge, noted that first the missionaries took our traditions, then the government, and now the hippies. Simultaneously the works of Black Elk, often referred to as the Native Bible, became popular. Due to the pan-Indianization of popular culture distinctions between Aboriginal traditions lessened and the New Age Movement evolved with the amalgamation of many teachings resulting in the loss of understanding each culture's uniqueness. This is the biggest threat to the validity of Aboriginal culture, spirituality and traditions. Aboriginal people struggle between sharing our traditions and keeping them to ourselves. Non-Aboriginal scientists are re-evaluating

Aboriginal understandings about the environment while we want to retain the validity of our own understandings and without having them translated by outsiders in ways that do not reflect our own patterns of thinking. For instance, Mohawk traditionalists teach people to collect plants for medicine by first showing the plant respect by placing some tobacco beside it and then asking the plant for permission to be taken. The spirit of the plant then informs the other plants that you are a respectful person; and only then will the other plants appear and the medicine work. Most other Aboriginal peoples would concur with this.

Oneida scholar, Pam Colorado (1988:50) uses the image of a tree to explain the concept of Aboriginal science as valid knowledge. She explains, "Like a tree the roots of Native Science goes deep into the history, body and blood of this land...In order for this understanding to occur, one must be a participant in a relationship with the tree." This is in contrast to Western notions of science where one does not participate in the science. Participation and experience are essential requirements for *Seeing the World with Aboriginal Eyes*. Personally, as a doctoral student, many of my experiences with elders from Mexico, Senegal, Hawaii, Arizona, Lappland and California were life transforming. For me, most important to that transformation was being rooted in my own lands and traditions, the *Kenienké: haka* (Mohawk).

Duality in Cosmology

Specific Aboriginal people view their world in unique ways. We Mohawks, have a duality in our cosmology based on twin brothers. We believe that the universe was in a state of continual tension and flux due to these twin brothers. The Twins, named *Teharonhiawako* and *Sawiskera*, were in a continual fight over who would control the world ever since their mother was killed. For example, *Teharonhiawako* would create the beauty of the rose and *Sawiskera* would then give it thorns. This fight over controlling earth is played out every year when *Sawiskera* brings winter and *Teharonhiawako* restores the earth in the spring. *Sawiskera's* name is derived from the root word ice while the nickname given *Teharonhia:wako* is sometimes sapling, just as a sapling shoots out in the spring. In Mayan cosmology, the twins, *Hanapu* and *Xblanque*, battle the lords of the underworld (Recinos *et al.*1950). In Navajo cosmology, twins battle the monsters that raged over the land (Navaho Curriculum Center 1971). The important cultural understanding to be gained from these stories is that the twins are needed to bring order and balance to the world they represent.

Teharonhiawako literally means "He who holds his head in

the sky" and is referred to as the right-handed twin, concerned with the things of the spirit and *Sawiskera*, is the left-handed twin concerned with controlling the earth. A contemporary application of this belief is that people controlling natural resources are influenced by *Sawiskera* and those working towards a sustainable world based on reciprocity and relationship are influenced by *Teharonhiawako*. Similar dualities are noted by Lakota psychologist, Ross (1989), who observes the right side of the brain deals with emotional and intuitive skills while the left side deals with analysis and logic. From the Rotinonshonni perspective we each hold an aspect of both twins; whether the Rotinonshonni or the western perspective is used, it is essential that we find a balance as a society between the two in order for us to make sure that we have a sustainable earth. This is a simplistic interpretation, time and effort is required to comprehend philosophical underpinnings imbedded in the actions, behaviors, traditions and beliefs of Aboriginal cultures. By *Seeing the World with Aboriginal Eyes*, we are attempting to interpret according to unique thinking patterns.

REALMS OF EXISTENCE

Aboriginal nations situate themselves within the universe in diverse ways that relate to their cosmologies and world views. Invariably, various realms of existence are present; for example, depending on the specific nation, the belief might be in an underworld, an earth world and a sky world. This section reveals connection between 'realms of existence' and the cosmologies and world views of Mi'kmaq, Beaver, Tewh, Cheyenne and Rotinonshonni. It explores how "realms of existence" shapes perceptions of reality.

Realms of Existence: What are they?

What do we mean when we speak about realms of existence? For Aboriginal peoples, realms of existence are those places accessed either through natural or supernatural means that provide meaning to everyday existence. They situate human and non-human persons within the cosmos. The most readily apparent realm of existence is that reality in which we live, breathe, and experience this earth. Other realms or dimensions are equally important to Aboriginal people. Each Aboriginal nation has its own world view, cosmology, and way of representing realms of existence. Generalizations are meaningless, however all Aboriginal cultures share the general concept of an underworld, a sky world, and a world on this earth. Additional realms of existence are located in each of these three main world concepts. This reality or physical dimension reflects the underworld and sky world (or other levels) with specific themes, such as being peopled by supernatural powers.

The Mi'kmaq universe includes six realms of existence: the world beneath the earth, the world beneath the water, the earth lodge, the ghost world, the sky world and the world beyond the stars (Henderson 1992). The circular earth lodge is situated at the center of the others. Algonquian peoples, such as the Mi'kmaq and Anishnawbe, pray in either four or seven directions: east, south, west and north, to the world below, to the world above, and to the center of human habitation (oneself). Lakota and other Aboriginal societies have similar realms, for example, Black Elk a Lakota medicine man, explained that it is to these directions that we must pray in each ceremony and thereby we create our own center of the universe (Brown 1990). Likewise, the Cheyenne cosmology, called *hestenov,* includes a multi-layered universe made of: *heammahstonev* above the earth, *Aktunov* below the earth, the atmosphere *taxtova* which surrounds the earth, *setova* above the atmosphere and above everywhere else *akotava.* Within each of these layers are the different aspects of Cheyenne cosmology such as spirit and terrestrial beings (Hoebel 1978). As well, the Tewa divide their cosmology into three realms with eight categories of persons living within them. These realms are surrounded by four sacred mountains. There is the *Sipofene* world known as *seht'a,* which is a term of tranference from the subtle world of *Sipohene* to the more dense world that the Tewa live in today (Ortiz 1975). These examples demonstrate the complexity of this topic; it is impossible to explain the breadth of cosmologies that exist within North American Aboriginal nations.

Concepts of Time

Other considerations to this complex topic are that of time and space, for these realms can exist simultaneously, be accessed through various means, be inhabited by supernatural and natural forces and provide a person with knowledge and talents that will help him/her live in this reality. These realms of existence are just as "real" and important to the believer as the physical realm and thus they can impact considerably on a person's life.

It is important to understand sacred, historical, mythological, and profane time, as well as the cyclical nature of time when exploring the realms of existence. For instance, when Aboriginal people speak about the world in which we live, we are often divided between sacred stories and historical stories. The sacred stories were interpreted by anthropologists as mythological stories. These include the stories of the archetypal hero and his relationship with the first beings of the world. Historical stories occurred are more contemporary.

Anishnawbe refer to sacred stories as *Atisokan* stories and historical stories as *Tibatchimowen* stories. Anishnawbe view *Atisokan* stories as part of their present reality; the sacred time of *Atisokan* stories occurs simultaneously with this reality. These stories are emergence stories that have to do with a transference from other realms of existence into the present earthly realm. They occur today as easily as they did when they were first presented after the first transference to this world by their archetypal ancestors. This is because *Atisokan* stories are placed in the context of what Eliade (1961) refers to as Great Sacred Time as opposed to profane time. It is by way of ceremony and the re-enacting of the cosmogony that a person may be projected into Great Sacred Time. Thus the telling of these stories is very crucial to the cosmology of each nation and, as a result, they are told during specific times of the year, such as the winter in order not to offend the resting spirits.

The cyclical nature of existence and how it relates to the concept of time within the various dimensions of existence needs to be explored as it becomes apparent that knowledge of the cycles of life and existence in this physical reality were and are critical to the renewal of life. These cycles in this reality are reflections of the sky world and underworld but are peopled by supernatural forces. Knowledge of these cycles of time assist people in accessing the various realms through spiritual means, such as vision quests, dreams, ceremonies and rituals.

The Mayans believed that by understanding the cycles of time, one could find the specific moments when sacred time and profane time converged. (Profane or secular time can be defined as the time in this present reality.) One of these cycles occurred every 52 years. Other cycles occurred every 52,000,000 years. As a result of this knowledge, the Mayans developed complex calendars based on mathematical formulas which foretold when these events occurred in the past and when they would happen again in the future. It was during these moments when sacred and profane time merged that ceremonies were held to renew the cyclical process of profane time so that life could continue on earth until this cycle ended and sacred and profane time came together again. The vision of sacred and profane time governs life in this reality just as it governs life in other dimensions of existence. Every 52 years the Mayans (Humbatzmen 1990) moved to other villages. Likewise, the Aztecs destroyed all of their possessions and began a new life at these times of convergence.

To put the cyclical nature of the world into contemporary thought, we just need to look at how the sky world informs the people in this physical dimension of knowledge. If this physical realm of existence is a reflection of the sky world, then knowledge of when actions take place up there, will be reflected on earth by the people living here. Consequently, an awareness of when the earth would be warm enough for plants to grow or when the annual migrations of birds and animals would take place was learned by the location of the stars. White (1990), for example, tells how his grandfather used these signs given to him by the environment to tell him how to live his traditional life. His grandfather had to be knowledgeable about every aspect of the environment in order to ensure that the generations to come would have a proper upbringing.

The Concept of Sacred Places

Another significant aspect that relates to realms of existence is the idea of sacred places. These are places on the earth that have a special connection to the other dimensions of existence. Mountains, for example, are considered sacred by many Aboriginal peoples and are often an integral part of their cosmology because they transcend this reality uniting the underworld, the earth, and the sky world and, thus, are present in the many realms that exist in their world view.

Deloria (1994) mentions the importance of sacred spaces to Aboriginal peoples. They are essential to defining the world in which we live. Ortiz (1978) also mentions the concept of sacred places through his explanation of the Tewa world, which is surrounded by four sacred mountains. Within the parameters of these four mountains live all the beings inhabiting their world, including the 'dry food people' who did not transform into the earth world, the Tewa and those who have been transformed into *xayeh* "stone."

These concepts of time, space, and the cyclical nature of existence persist in the various realms of existence. Many Aboriginal peoples have devised unique ways of depicting their understanding of the cosmos, often described with a circle and the four directions. For many Aboriginal peoples, such as the Cree and Anishnawbe, the four directions lie within the parameter of the circle. The Beaver represent the four directions as a cross within a circle. The Lakota have the same representation with the cross signifying the four directions and the circle infinity. Each Aboriginal society defines what the directions represent based on their own cultural understandings. For example, for the Beaver the east is sunrise and represents *Duneza* (Real People) where the animals return in the spring to be hunted again; the south symbolizes warmth and nurturance when the sun is at its mid-day point; the west, represents darkness where the sun sets, and the north is viewed as night when the sun no longer appears.

The Connection between the Various Realms of Existence

What connects these various realms of existence? What allows the forces of these realms to enter this reality and the people to access the other realms? In some Aboriginal cultures the linkage of these realms is via a cosmic pillar whereas in others, the connection is by a great celestial tree some refer to as the World Tree of Life. In the cultures in which the celestial tree is part of the cosmology, it is noted that the roots lead to the under world, the trunk is a part of the earth world, while branches of the tree reach into the sky world. In addition, the celestial tree is at the center of the dimensional worlds and acts as a channel. Thus, it is the channel that connects the physical realm of existence with the metaphysical realms of existence for its parts exist in all the worlds.

The celestial tree, the connection to the supernatural powers, and the other realms, represents the archetypal tree of all other trees. For the Mi'kmag, the tree's roots flow into the deep earth realm and up to the root world and earth world realms. Its trunk then reaches from the earth world into the sky world. In Rotinonshonni cosmology, a Dew Eagle is placed on top of the tree, transcending the lower worlds and traveling to the highest world of the spirit. Aboriginal nations represent the celestial tree in their cosmology with a tree species that is important to their existence. For instance, the Anishnawbe represented the celestial tree with the cedar; the Rotinonshonni represented it with the white pine; The Dakota with a cotton wood, and the Mayan people used the Ceiba.

Often complex teachings accompany the celestial tree. For example, it is first presented in Rotinonshonni cosmology as existing in the sky world before the transference of the Great Beings to the earth world. On top of this celestial tree is the Hagaks' Great Dew Eagle who watches over the children of creation. He gives the children in the sky world their instructions and can be called upon when they are in trouble. After the transference of the cosmological beings to Turtle Island (North America) and the beginning of humanity the understandings of the cosmic order are lost. They are restored when the Rotinonshonni go through a period of great strife, and the celestial tree, represented as the Great White Pine with an eagle placed on top to watch over the people, is re-established by the *Peacemaker* at the center of their world, at *Kanat: kowa* village, Onondaga. The Onondaga being one of the Five Original confederated nations of the Rotinonshonni. The *Peacemaker* re-established the connection with other realms for the Rotinonshonni in order to end strife, with the eagle watching over, and Onondaga became the spiritual centre of the Rotinonshonni world view on earth. Therefore, in order to connect with the other realms one must be a practitioner of a way of life based on the *Peacemaker*'s teachings, called the *Keyaneren: Kowa.*

Beings exist within the different realms of existence; beings who are not on the earth plane are referred to by their spiritual nature such as *Manitou* by the Anishnawbe, *Oia:ron* by the Rotinonshonni, *T'owa* by the Tewa, and *Maiyu* by the Cheyenne. Other Aboriginal peoples including the Beaver, refer to these beings as their grandfathers (Mills 1992). For all these Aboriginal peoples, the other-than-human beings provide focus and direction to the people on earth and assist them in their daily activities in this realm of existence. These beings speak to the people through dreams, vision quests, special rituals, and ceremonies. These beings may enter this realm of existence just as specially trained persons can enter the other metaphysical realms that they inhabit.

Creation Stories and Prophecies

Now that we have explored the concept of realms of existence, the existence of sacred time and place within these realms, the connecting capacity of the celestial tree or cosmic pillar, and the presence of other-than-human beings in these realms, we need to examine how creation stories and prophecies fit into this way of describing the cosmos. Creation stories inform people of the beginnings of the physical realm of existence in which they live while prophecies foretell changes to this physical dimension. Commonalities exist in many Aboriginal cultures' creation stories, even though these societies may be separated by thousands of miles. The Dené in the Northwest, the Rotinonshonni in the Northeast, and the Algonquian peoples of the eastern subarctic all tell the story of how the animals replenish the earth after a great flood occurs. Referred to as the earth diver story, the land/water animals dive below the sea to look for some earth to place on the back of a turtle so that they can return to live on land. The otter dives first and is unsuccessful; then the beaver dives and fails; finally the least of the land/water beings, the muskrat, dives and successfully finds some earth and places it on the turtle's back, thus, providing a place to live and the creation of this physical realm of existence.

The teachings presented in our creation stories inform us of the creation of our physical realm of existence as well as where human beings are situated in relation to other life forms. The teachings explain that human beings are the most dependent on the other beings and have the fewest natural abilities; human beings were created last, we are the younger brother who needs guidance from others to survive. Traditionally, many Aboriginal peoples rated the natural world by the natural abilities rather than the intelligence of various species. Waterfowl were rated the highest because they had the ability to fly, swim, and live on land. The land/water animals, such as the otter, beaver and muskrat, were rated next, due to their abilities to inhabit both land and water and finally, the land-based animals, including humans, were considered among the least able. Human beings have to utilize everything in the natural world to survive; other animals give of themselves to help weaker siblings survive. These abilities are also transferable to the spirit realms. Thus the human being is very limited and in need of special help in order to transgress the different spiritual realms.

Human beings received direction from their dreams and from animal's help through vision fasts, called *muyine* by the Beaver. Fur trader, George Nelson, mentioned Anishnawbe learned about medicinal plants through their dreams. There was a place they traveled to in their dreams when they needed medicines. At the center of this place was a great mountain. Growing along the mountain were all of the plants needed for medicines. Teachers or specialists taught dreamers about plant uses and awakening, the dreamer would have knowledge about a particular plant and its use as a medicine (Brown & Brightman 1999). Often, their spirit helpers would aid dreamers when going on their journeys. Some dreamers learned to metamorphose into their spirit helpers and took the form of a bird to travel.

Through dreams we develop special relationships with the entities in other realms. This ability is required through fasting. Have you ever had a dream where you feel awake and can't move. The reason this occurs is your conscious spirit has left your body and is having trouble returning. The same occurs when fasting. Our dreams during the fast allow us to travel to the different realms where we encounter different spirit entities. The difference between an experienced faster and person having a waking dream, is the faster learns how to control the dream. He can make relationships and alliances with those he meets in the dream. He becomes aware of everything in the dream. It is in our dreams that we learn sacred knowledge; are given songs; and meet others that have passed from this world. Cree elders like Louis Bird refer to this as *Miteo*. Those who learn to dream can do so for weeks at a time, requiring little food or water. They slow down their metabolism, like bears hibernating in the winter.

Prophecies also have an integral role in this exploration into the various realms of existence. Many prophecies foretell changes to the realm which people inhabit on a daily basis. For instance, Aboriginal societies believe that this world is coming to an end. The Rotinonshonni foretold in the early nineteenth century that the signs of this change will occur when the tops of the trees begin to dry and the waters become poisoned. The Anishnawbe believe that an Eighth Fire will be lit that will bring destructive forces if the non-Aboriginal peoples do not change their ways. For Aboriginal peoples, these changes simply result in a transition from this reality into another, an emergence into another world or realm of existence. Many Aboriginal peoples' prophecies mention four pre-existing worlds from which they emerged when the balance in the world was lost. The realms of existence are ever-changing throughout the duration of the earth. Life is cyclical in nature and ever transforming.

Controversy exists on how to interpret prophecies that relate to the end of the world or the transformation of this reality into another form. Some Aboriginal and non-Aboriginal peoples interpret prophecies to mean that global changes will affect them literally. Others interpret prophecies to mean that when Aboriginal culture and ceremonies are no longer practiced their world will come to an end, along with the demise of their cultural world view. All believe that through the continuance of our ceremonies we help keep the world in balance. We are direct participants in the continuance of a healthy world. Both interpretations indicate concerns over the sustainability of the earth, the world-wide adoption of the western capitalist world view, and the need to retain Aboriginal philosophies in order to maintain this current reality. For many, there are grave signs indicating a change in this reality. For example, although many Aboriginal communities have successfully developed a monetary based economy, it is not always a social success. Communities such as *Hobema*, Alberta and *Passamaquoddy*, Maine have extremely high suicide rates among their young people and are looking at ways to balance traditional sustainable economic systems with their newly acquired wealth. Adamson (1992) believes that the only way to alleviate these social problems is by finding long term solutions based on traditional values, which Christian clergy now dominating many Aboriginal communities are unwilling to allow. To perpetuate the current realm of existence, original teachings and values given at the time of creation need to be restored and revitalized. Cornelius (1992) explains how the process may begin with the Thanksgiving address of the Rotinonshonni, which gives thanks to all of creation. This is a teaching about our relationships to the environment that all societies could learn from and adopt.

VISION AND SOUND

Each culture has a unique way of interpreting the world around them and understanding and deciphering the sounds they hear and the sights they see based on Aboriginal peoples' traditions, beliefs, spirituality and teachings. Cyclical time is explored in greater depth, the relationship of traditions to the concept of sound, art, music and language is discussed, as well as how all these are connected to each other. A spiritual and metaphysical approach is used as the exploration into these themes delves into the belief patterns and ways of knowing of various Aboriginal peoples of North America.

How We Sense our World

Can people from differing cultures actually see and hear in different ways? Is it possible to understand the sounds and sights of the universe on levels that are distinct and unique? There are multitudes of phenomena that are not fully understood and just as many ways of interpreting them that are culturally specific. The abilities of seeing and hearing are culturally distinct and depend on a person's orientation to the cosmos. How do the senses affect our perception of the world? In what ways do we interpret what we see and hear through the influences of culture? Although there are many diverse Aboriginal cultures worldwide, each with their own language, beliefs, and traditions, there are also commonalities, just as the world views of many European peoples share common features. Therefore, I will focus on the broader spectrum rather than confining this discussion to aspects that are narrow and limiting.

Circles, Cycles and Spirals

Many scholars note that viewing time in a linear manner is a fairly recent occurrence as most primal civilizations, including those in Europe, oriented their lives to natural cycles (Brown 1982). Changes due to industrialization and urbanization have shifted orientation on cyclical time to linear time; although Aboriginal peoples continue to orient themselves according to these ancient and original patterns of thought and many still follow the patterns set by the rhythms of nature as it cycles through time. For instance, the Mayans followed this cyclical time frame, developing elaborate calendars reflecting the movements of the sun, moon, planets and stars, including the entire cosmos within their cultural orientation. Unlike the calendar of Euro-western peoples that reflects the specific actions of humans (Easter, Canada Day, Labour Day, Christmas, Valentine's Day, etc.), the Mayan calendar was a sophisticated and complex plan that reflected humankind's relation and connection to the universe. This allowed daily activities to be practiced in harmony with the universe rather than in a plan set arbitrarily by human precepts. The calendar of the Mayans was based on sacred and profane time. It governed the dates when ceremonies and rituals were practiced and how they were performed.

The most common calendar was a continually repeated 13 day cycle intersected by a 20 day calendar with each day represented by a different name. As each cycle of twenty ended, it repeated itself, beginning at the second number of the 13 day calendar. It took 13 revolutions and 260 days to complete the cycle before the same number and name could reoccur. The Mayans referred to the 260 day calendar as their *tsolkin* calendar (Jones & Jones 1995). Another Mayan calendar had 365 days divided by 18 HAAB periods containing 20 days each, making a 360 day calendar with five extra days for special ceremonies (Jones & Jones 1995). These five days added up over time and became part of the calendar cycle of 260 *tsolkin* days. There were 13 periods every 52 years which were important times of renewal for the Mayans. At the beginning of each cycle, the earth was in configuration with all the planets and the planets began a new cosmic cycle. Within these cycles, the Mayans embraced all aspects of their secular and spiritual lives, integrating the sacred and the profane. Even today, during a recent configuration of the planets, Mayan elders came to *Chichen Itza*, in the Yucatan to witness this event and to pray for another renewal of a 52 year cycle.

While in the Traditional Knowledge Program, Humbatzmen (1990) explained calendars and cycles at the ancient Mayan sacred sites. Humbatzmen (1990) is one of the few Mayans allowed on these sacred sites. After much lobbying by him the Mexican government acknowledged Humbatzmen's knowledge as a possible tourist attraction and allowed him to guide tours at ancient Mayan sites. My only criticism of his approach was the use of spiritual language acquired from northern New Agers looking for a spiritual guru. Nonetheless, visiting ancient Mayan sites with a Mayan, rather than with a Mexican tour guide was an enriching experience.

Like the Mayans, other Aboriginal peoples based their way

of life on cycles; the dominating cycles of the natural world and the universe varied from culture to culture. For example, the Mayans were an agricultural nation that based their planting and harvesting on the solstice and equinox cycles. Hunting cultures based their lives on the migratory and reproductive cycles of wild game. Seeing time as a pattern of cycles imparts a unique perspective forming the basis of a society's activities on their particular view of the universe. The concept of cyclical time within a cultural world view forms the foundation for the supporting traditions, beliefs and actions. In addition, whenever individuals from this cultural worldview watch the stars, ocean tides, sun, or moon, they are vividly aware of the perpetual motion described by the cycles of the universe and its relationship to their own lives. Traditional Aboriginal people understand that the universe is in perpetual motion and ever expanding in the creation of new forms of life. Anishnawbe and Mayans compare the universe to either a spiral ever extending outward or a cyclical spiral motion. Through this cyclical spiral motion of the universe, the working of *Hunab K'u*, the Creator, can be understood. This concept of the universe as a spiral that continually revolves and the Creator as a continual process of motion emanating outwards has implications reflected in spiritual beliefs, language, songs, and the visual arts. What people see and hear on the metaphysical and inner levels is expressed through speech, music, and art.

This is clearly demonstrated through Aboriginal languages. The majority of Aboriginal languages are verb-based whereas languages from European traditions are noun-based. This becomes significant when speaking of all-encompassing spiritual forces, for unlike Euro-western traditions in which God is viewed as a person and described with a stationary noun, Aboriginal traditions such as the Mayan, view the Creator and his creation in perpetual motion and translate this concept into verbs of movement and measure. The idea of motion and activity is presented whenever verbs are spoken and influences all aspects of speech from the most mundane to the most profound.

The cyclical dynamic nature of existence and the universe is believed by many Aboriginal peoples. It extends into many of our creation stories, cosmologies, and our spiritual beliefs. We see this concept of cycles as well as belief patterns relating to sight and sound. For example, the Anishnawbe and Mayans envision the Milky Way as a spiral, as well as a path of souls. Following this path, a soul could reach the place where sound first had its beginnings within the spiral of the universe. The sound that emanated from the beginning of the universe is the primal sounds of the cosmos. At the portion of the universe that protrudes outward vibrations emit sounds heard by our inner being, unheard by our ears. The sounds we hear with our ears are known from the physical world, sounds heard by our inner being are sounds of the other realms of existence.

Sound and Song

The connection of sound to the spiral of the universe is understood in the Anishnawbe creation story, *The Seven Fires of the Ojibway Nation* recorded by a *Midewiwin* spiritual leader (Benton-Banai 1979). Before the universe was formed there was only silence and darkness. Then, a sound began emanating from somewhere in the centre of the void and began to carry outward. In the centre where the sound first began was the Creator. This sound is referred to as the First Fire. The Creator then sent his thoughts in every direction, leaving stars and light in a flaming spiral called the Second Fire. Emitting from this spiral of fire came all the qualities that bring life: the seasons, the winds, the four directions, the sun and the moon. This is called the Third Fire. Next, all the components of the universe were set in a circular motion, which is called the Fourth Fire. Then the first to arrive were the winged peoples and this is called the Fifth Fire. Then earth was made woman with the raindrops her tears and the lakes and streams her blood. From her body evolved the many other forms of life that exist: the four-leggeds, the swimmers, the standing peoples... and this is called the Sixth Fire. Finally, the Creator took handfuls of dirt from Mother Earth and from her made the first human being and this is called the Seventh Fire. This is a very brief synopsis of the Anishnawbe creation story, the fact pertinent to this discussion is that sound radiated from the centre of the void and was first and foremost a part of the creative process of the universe. For the Anishnawbe this primal sound of creation is symbolized in the sound of the Little Boy Water Drum, described as having the same sound as the heart beat of the universe, representing the ever expanding spiral universe.

Other Aboriginal traditions also tell of sacred primal sounds. For the Mayans, sounds and creation are closely connected, bridging people with the creative forces of the universe. The O, G and T sounds are sacred. When the Mayans use the sound O, they add an L after it so it sounds like OL. The sound O stands for awakened conscious while L stands for vibration. The Hindus of India use the same concept while meditating on the sound OM. The sound G represents the egg, Creator of the universe's germination seed. For Anishnawbe, the G sound is named as the First Fire of Creation. In Mayan hieroglyphics, the sound is represented in the symbol of a spiral, the same as the symbol for the galaxy or Milky Way. The sound T represents the sacred tree, the

Ceiba, a symbol of the World Tree connecting supernatural powers with the physical realm of existence. The sacred tree also represents the consciousness that unites all the cosmic laws and is referred to as *Teol* by the Mayans.

Another example of the presence and significance of primal sounds is explained by the Aztec Musician, Mazalt Golindo (1996), a teacher in the Traditional Knowledge Program, who says sacred sounds used in ceremonies are produced by singing two notes simultaneously. Between these two sounds, lies a third sound which connects a person to one of the energy realms of existence. This well traveled musician learned the meaning of this sound from an Indigenous Hill people in China. The Tibetan Lamas utilize this same technique in their meditations and chants. Although not an elder, Mazalt Golindo (1996) is a unique and gifted person. He picked up a guitar and began busking in Mexico City; becoming so proficient he played flute with professional Aboriginal musician Robbie Robertson. Then Mazalt Golindo decided to become a painter, now his art work is highly sought after. Today Golindo is a cultural ambassador for the Indigenous people of Mexico. His mother is a highly regarded matriarch of the Indigenous people of Mexico City.

In many traditional Aboriginal cultures everything that exists and is considered alive can be represented by primal sounds, the sound is more important than the name. These primal sounds exist in languages of the people and in the sounds emitted by the universe. Within these sounds is a power and energy that can be tapped by those who can access them. Aboriginal languages are based on word meaning as well as word sounds which place one in relationship with the different aspects of creation. Henderson (1992) says every Indigenous language has sounds connected to the different realms that make up the cosmology. For example, to hear the Haida speak is to listen to the waves on the shore and the cry of the birds (Peat 1994). When Anishnawbe call the thunders it is the name, *animikeek*, and its thunderbird sound that is important (Smith 1991). The importance of sound is seen in children's names which are based on the dream experience of an elder who meets the *manitouk* of the child's namesake in a dream. The names of children are connected by sound to nature giving the names a strength and energy of nature. Words derive energy and potency from the sounds that are embodied in the words. Hearing or speaking words and sounds introduces another way of hearing outside the physical realm that has far reaching implications in all aspects of daily physical and spiritual existence.

Often sounds in songs related to the various forces of existence.

For instance, the drum beat is described as the heart beat of Mother Earth; songs of Aboriginal words sound like the ocean, the whispering winds, and the murmur of trees speaking with the Creator. Sounds and songs are an entranceway to communicating with supernatural forces. Often these songs are learned from the energies and forces of nature tapped into during vision quests, dreams, and special ceremonies. Knowing these songs can link a person with the Creator and the forces of life, if a person knows the sound or song of a power of nature, then that power can assist and support the person. Carpenter (1978) adds that it is the music which cannot be heard by the ear which is the very essence of the vision quest. Henderson (1992) says these personal sounds are rarely spoken or sung. Traditionally, knowing these sounds and songs was crucial to a successful life and a strong Aboriginal nation; therefore, use of sacred songs and sounds was highly scrutinized.

Songs are important to the Anishnawbe, Rotinonshonni, and Navajo. The Anishnawbe painted birch bark scrolls with red ochre to record songs using mystical representation of sounds. Songs were given by the powers of nature and the supernatural forces; they belonged solely to the person to whom they were given and could only be used under certain conditions by particular people. Great care and judgment had to be exercised regarding the singing of some songs as powers might be blunted if used inappropriately. The Rotinonshonni spoke while creating their wampum belts. When reciting the meaning of the belt, they ask the belt to help them remember the words. Kenienké haka (Mohawk) traditionalists say that everything has a song. When the medicine plant gives you its song, you are sure to benefit from its medicine. Every person has their own *Adowa* (song) learned either by being handed down or in a vision quest. The *Adowa* is sung when one is about to pass from this world so the guiding spirits can identify individuals on their journey to the spirit world. The Navaho create elaborate sand mandalas based on sacred formulae. An ailing person is placed on the mandala, sacred healing songs are sung, and then the medicine person destroys the mandala, which sweeps the person's sickness away.

Powers of Nature Communicating with People

Within many Aboriginal teachings other-than-human persons, such as plants and animals, can be spoken to by humans and understood when they speak to a human. Sometimes *Manitouk* (spirits of these unseen forces) such as the Thunders, are there to assist healers. The powers of nature communicating with people is related in a story told by an Anishnawbe man from Manitoulin Island whose son had been ill since birth. While a *Cree* medicine man was visiting a thunderstorm suddenly appeared, lasted about five minutes, and suddenly disappeared. The Anishnawbe man mentioned this storm to the *Cree* medicine man who replied that Thunders were his helpers who aided him in healing; the *Cree* medicine man knew the sounds of the Thunders and how to summon them. Another example is found in the story of the "First Twins" who call the *Kachinas;* arriving in thunder they bring hope and peace to the *Tewa* people (Velarde 1989). A final example of communicating with nature is found in an Anishnawbe elder's story. The elder worked in the uranium mines and was later diagnosed with cancer. One day he was compelled to kneel by a tree in his yard, hug it and pray in his original language, asking it for help. While in the cancer ward of the hospital a strange woman appeared and told him he would be all right. From that moment on, his cancer began receding. When he returned home the tree he had knelt by and spoke to, had turned yellow and began to die.

These stories may be difficult for some to comprehend. Those who understand that sounds have power beyond the physical realm and that one can communicate with thunder and other helping forces within the universe, realize that these stories are credible. Relating these stories may open an unfamiliar area of human existence that informs how the spiritual senses operate in tangent with the physical senses, and how the spiritual sense of sound goes back into primordial time when the universe was created. The holistic understanding of cycles and sound may never be fully attained as many Aboriginal nations were forced to adopt other languages, to forsake the ways of the past, or are now extinct. Understanding cycles and sound is critical to *Seeing the World with Aboriginal Eyes* as the traditions and teachings are an integral part of the knowledge and thought patterns held within Aboriginal cultures.

THE WORLD OF THE SPIRIT

Forces and powers exist within all aspects of the universe. Those who are specially trained or seek the help of medicine persons or guardian spirits may tap into this power to lighten the vicissitudes of life, to help others, or to achieve a sense of oneness with the universe. Everyone is given natural power, spiritual power is available through dreams, trances, ceremonies, chants, vision quests, and other activities. *Seeing the World with Aboriginal Eyes* requires an understanding of powers and forces in the universe other than those expressed by the five senses, which are experienced on other levels of human existence.

Aboriginal Understandings of Powers and Forces in the Universe

Powers and forces are vibrating at a quicker pace than the forces we are aware of in the dimension in which we live. These energies reside in us and we can add to them by tapping into other energy sources. Lakota elder, Frank Fools Crow, as written by Thomas Mails (1991), described this energy as spiritual power, or *Wakan*, which is absorbed by the healer and used only in specific ways. The powers residing in these energies are called *Wakan* (Lakota), *Orenta* (Rotinonshonni), and *Manitou* (Anishnawbe). The Anishnawbe say the *Manitou,* or spiritual forces, reside along side the physical realm and can be accessed by anyone with the proper knowledge. Stories about the time when everyone communicated with animals refer to communicating with the *Manitou* of the animal world. As agriculturalists, the Rotinonshonni were heavily involved with the plant world, communicating with the spiritual forces of the plant world. *Orenta* is the energy and power that exits within everything on both the earthly and spiritual planes.

The Rotinonshonni, Anishnawbe, Lakota and many other Aboriginal nations have a similar understanding of spiritual power. We *onkwe honwe* (real people) and members of the Rotinonshonni believe that certain youth acquired *Orenta* and became noted healers during their puberty fast. This was referred to as being hidden under the husk of corn and the chosen youth were required to remain chaste even after the puberty fast was over. The Rotinonshonni's force opposing the healing energies of *Orenta* is *Otkon,* which is the energy for selfish or malevolent purposes. Harmony and balance occur by holding two opposing forces in tension, including male/female, day/night, sun/moon, and *Orenta/Otkon.*

Places on earth where the energy levels are more pronounced and accessible to humankind are sacred places on earth. Many religions from other cultures have a similar concept and build religious centres at equivalent locations. At Aboriginal sacred places, knowledgeable individuals obtain additional powers for healing, wisdom, and enlightenment required for specific feats or dilemmas in life. For the Rotinonshonni there are places where the *Peacemaker* visited that are sacred. For example, while writing my dissertation I visited the war trail that *Jokansasee* (Mother of Nations) lived on in the *Tuscarora* reservation in New York State, across from the Niagara River. Another sacred place I visited was Cohoes Falls where the *Peacemaker* pacified the Kenienké: haka war chiefs, giving them good minds. Another sacred place is at *Onondaga*, where the rock is located that *Tadadaho* sat on when he called out to the nations thousands of years ago. Similarly, the Gitksan in British Columbia, are connected to the spiritual power of their ancestral lands. This is represented through their clan songs, stories and totems, which link people to the spirit power so that "man, spirit power and the land ... form a living whole." (Knudtson & Suzuki 1992). The Lakota in South Dakota access sacred power at specific sites in the Black Hills. For example, at the top of Harney Peak when certain constellations are correctly positioned, people perform ceremonies to access the spiritual powers. The Anishnawbe elders in the Sudbury, Ontario region identify sacred places in the LaCloche Mountains where they access to the realm of spiritual forces after a four day fast. While fasting, some of the power and forces of the region are revealed; however, to access these energies one must be purified in a Sweat Lodge Ceremony prior to fasting. As one becomes weaker in body during the fast, he or she becomes stronger in spirit. Other times that one is stronger or closer to the spirit world is as a very young child and as a very old adult; as an Anishinawbe elder stated, the closer to death, the closer you will be to the spirit world – the realm of this spiritual power. Near death is the time when contact is made between the natural world of this reality and the unseen intangible dimension of the spirit world. Death is the time when the soul makes its final passage over to this spiritual realm, along with the power given to each life form.

The Mayans in Central America have similar beliefs about spiritual power (Humbatzmen 1990). In the land of the Mayan, there are seven energy centres located on Earth in line with the constellations, sun or moon. At these sacred sites, ceremonies are held on behalf of the resident deities. These sacred places create a continuity that brings together the past and the present (Deloria 1994); providing a social cohesion with their ancestry. Also, there are seven energy points in the human body and humans can become *Quezalcoatl* or *Kukulcan,* the Giver of Movement and Measure. Once the significance of energy points is understood by an individual and s/he is in harmony with these energy centres, an individual can access this spiritual power. This theme is also found in other ancient religions throughout the world.

Seeing the World with Aboriginal Eyes involves comprehending intangible aspects of the universe. These powers and forces vibrate at a more rapid rate than that in which we live and have been known for eons to be an important part of Earth. These sources of powers reside in humankind and in animate beings surrounding humankind. They are referred to as *Wakan* (Lakota), *Orenta* (Iroquois) and *Manitou* (Anishnawbe).

Chapter Two

SOUTHERN DOOR:
WAYS OF RELATING

Relationships among all beings, whether they are spiritual or tangible, is one aspect of Aboriginal spiritual thought throughout North America. These relationships are embodied in the expression "All My Relations." In this expression people acknowledge their relationships with other humans, the other-than-humans, the animals and plants, the land, and the forces and powers of the cosmos (seen and unseen) so that spiritual and physical well-being is maintained. This chapter explores spiritual concepts uniting humankind with the cosmos, how this unity is accomplished, and how this connection with the cosmos is reflected in perceptual orientation.

How Aboriginal Peoples Relate to Our World

Aboriginal people have a holistic '360 degree' perspective of the world (Dumont 1997) that sees the unity of the universe by connecting giving and receiving relationships. Complementary and mutual links between each part of the cosmos form an interconnected web. Aboriginal people are connected to this web by the sacredness that exists in all things. For example, for the Anishnawbe everything is a result of the creative power of *Kitchi Manitou,* which is inherent in all living things (Jenness 1935), connects all things in the universe, and provides Aboriginal peoples with their world views. *Kitchi Manitou* is the energy from whom all things evolve and with whom all things exist in balance. This energy keeps order in the universe. Aboriginal peoples refer to the order and harmony existing at the time of creation as the original instructions. To maintain a balanced world each aspect of creation is given instructions to follow – the sun rises in the east and sets in the west; birds migrate and constellations appear and disappear at certain times of the year; and the moon follows a monthly cycle. When one of these cycles falters the rest of creation is affected. Each segment of the universe depends on another so each element of the cosmos must play its role to avoid cataclysmic consequences.

Aboriginal people play their role in maintaining harmony and balance by expressing and supporting the laws of nature that unite them with the cosmos through ceremonies and ritualistic observances. The sun and other beings in the universe see non-participation in these important activities as disrespectful, resulting in consequences such as the sun not rising or giving warmth. As described for a Pipe Ceremony, "For what ever reason the act was performed, it was always done with reverence and holiness" (Johnston 1882: 33). Aboriginal people are the link ensuring balance is maintained in the world, this and the fact that humans are one with everything is the foundation of ceremonies and rites (Brown 1969). As expressed in the Sweat Lodge ceremony individuals carry the universe both metaphorically and literally:

> The *Onikare* or Sweat Lodge of the Lakota is a
> means whereby the elements of water, fire, earth
> and air are all linked in a communicative discourse
> with the person(s) holding the sweat. These elements
> are examples that teach us. The water, for instance,
> is always flowing and giving life. The fire is the
> powerful centre of all things. The rocks represent the
> earth as something indestructible. The steam from
> the heated rocks represents the sacred breath of life
> (Brown 1969: 31).

Water, fire, earth and air, plus the people conducting the Sweat Lodge ceremony are linked in a purification right. The four elements are acknowledged for their power, which is utilized for the benefit of the people holding the sweat. These elements can also destroy people who are disrespectful. This ceremony reinforces the connections between individuals and the universe; the universe becomes a part of the participant's being and participants become a part of the universe, linked for eternity. Through such ceremonies Aboriginal people utilize knowledge received from all aspects of creation and received from their original instructions to become participants with all beings and powers leading a harmonious life cycle with all other facets of the universe.

In *Seeing the World with Aboriginal Eyes,* it is understood that one receives as much as that person gives. Selfish individuals end up with nothing, or harming themselves and their families. This reciprocal relationship is developed from early childhood and is critical to ones ability to reach *pimadaziwin,* an Anishnawbe term meaning 'life to the fullest' or elderhood. The Anishnawbe for example, develop reciprocal relationships with their guiding spiritual forces, sometimes referred to as *Pawaganak,* by fasting for four days. During the fast, intuitive skills needed to connect with the more subtle spiritual forces looking after all living things in the physical world become more acute. Once one opens to the spiritual realms of the *Manitou* and *Pawaganak,* he or she is contacted directly or through dreams to a *Pawagan* who guides human beings on Earth and is connected to the souls of animals, plants, water beings and the cosmological bodies such as the sun, moon or winds. Once the relationship is formed with the *Pawagan,* it becomes a lifelong guiding spirit helper. Obligations and sacrifices in the form of offerings and thanks are made to the helper to ensure that both parties benefit from these relationships. For example, through dreams the *Pawagan* guides hunting activities which are reciprocated with feasts or tobacco. The lack of these offerings could make a *Pawagan* bring starvation or death. The link existing in all things, in both the natural and spiritual world, enables the *Pawaganak* to metamorphose and appear as human beings, just as a conjurer can metamorphose into animal form (Hallowell 1967).

The Naskapi living in the subarctic are guided by a spiritual force called *Ate'k'wabe'o* (Caribou Man) who ensures that only so many caribou allow themselves to be offered to a hunter. Conjurers can visit *Ate'k'wabe'o* and receive instructions. If instructions are followed they are rewarded, disobeying instructions could result in loosing ones conjuring power for up to a year (Speck 1963). Hunter's responsibility to the caribou is to use all parts of the animal, to waste part of a caribou entices the wrath of *Ate'k'wabe'o* and result in starvation (Speck 1963). Other animal spirits, including the bear and beaver, must also be appeased by following ritualistic observances to maintain balance and harmony. A most important spirit of the Naskapi is the soul spirit referred to as *Mista'peo* (Big Man). Hunters must develop a relationship with his own *Mista'peo* to live a full life (Dumont 1997).

The environment also plays an important role in determining which spirits are in control. For example, for the Naskapi living in the subarctic, the leader of the animal spirits is the bear. For the Cree living on the prairies, the leader of the spirits is the buffalo. Aboriginal societies orient their cultures to the beings around them (Hallowell 1967). They learn their cosmological orientation through the species and forces of nature they associate with and that are essential to their existence.

Within a society's space are the corporeal and non-corporeal beings with whom people develop their relationships. They must first name the topological features, identify which places are sacred, and know which ones are within their boundaries. Every Aboriginal territory consists of sacred areas, which are approached in a certain manner, such as offering tobacco. Sacred places are like spirit realms, which are only entered using a specific behaviour to establish a reciprocal relationship with the powers and forces of that area (Hallowell 1967),

Understanding the importance of sacred space, informs Aboriginal people that there are boundaries in the world which cannot normally be transgressed. In certain circumstances and with the help of spirits, these areas may be accessed in dreams, visions or through the help of spiritual teachers (shamans). Some sacred places are inhabited by spirits, animals and even other human beings who have developed their own world view rendering these territories out of bounds.

Aboriginal societies never looked at each other as being one homogenous society inhabiting the same space, each Aboriginal society interpreted phenomena in their world through their own unique cultural understandings. For example, although the Anishnawbe and Rotinonshonni viewed the same movement of the star constellations, sun and moon, they interpreted these movements with their own cultural understandings of human and non-human beings inhabiting the universe. Each Aboriginal society has their own original instructions. To transgress the boundaries of another society might result in being punished by corporeal or non-corporeal beings residing in the area.

These rules also applied to persons living in the same society. Among the Anishnawbe a family was a steward of an area and responsible for maintaining a balance within the parameters of their territory. Family territories were bordered by natural formations such as mountains or lakes. They knew how many animals inhabited the area and their gender. The length of their territory was measured by how many times they slept before reaching their destination or by the sun's position (Hallowell 1967). Strict rules governed the territories of each family and proper respect was shown prior to entering another family's territory. This ensured sustainable resource usage and that reciprocal relationships made with spirits were respected. Interlopers could affect the balance of reciprocal relationships resulting in retribution from spirits, which could cause harm to the family. These rules were not to protect ownership of one's private property, as land could not be owned.

Finally, Aboriginal peoples in general oriented their activities by following the cycles of nature which also established reciprocal arrangements. For instance, they planned their activities around the 13 monthly cycles of the moon. Each lunar cycle was named after a natural occurrence during a particular cycle, such as the migration of birds or the sprouting of certain plants. Star constellations appeared at certain times of the year and used as reference points for activities such as hunting and planting. Non-hunting periods occurred when animals were bearing their young and correlated with certain constellations appearing during that period.

Plants for medicine were picked during the full moon when they are most mature. By following these cyclical observations people's relationships with the natural world were honoured. Links between different beings and the activities they perform in the world and the universe were consistently respected. This web of life, in which all are related in special and unique ways, forms the foundational belief pattern of Aboriginal societies, for no one item ever acts independently. Each being helps to inform the other of their link to each other. This concept of interrelationships is represented in the sacred Rotinonshonni medicines known as the Little Water, which according to Thomas (1990), requires over a hundred ingredients consisting of plant and animal life. It is through such examples that we can truly understand the importance of relationships, for in the case of this medicine all ingredients must be working together in harmony to make the medicine effective.

Throughout this section, the importance of reciprocity has been stressed; nothing will function properly unless reciprocity is fostered and maintained. This applies to all areas of existence and is based on the laws of nature and the cosmos that unite humankind with the physical and non-physical beings.

RELATIONSHIPS WITH THE EARTH WORLD

Aboriginal beliefs that refer to humankind's relation to the earth world, the plant and animal peoples and the environment are examined in this section. Respect, reciprocity, sharing, balance and harmony are a few of the themes discussed, along with how patterns of thought on ones relationship with the Earth world is promoted in daily lives.

How Aboriginal People Relate to Earth

In order to *See the World with Aboriginal Eyes,* there has to be a sense of oneness with Earth. This sense of oneness is promoted and fostered through various cultural mechanisms, including teachings, traditional stories, ceremonies, rites and traditions integrated into all aspects of their daily lives. The values are seen on a daily basis. Daily behaviour patterns reinforcing human relationships with the natural world have emerged, reflecting the beliefs found within these traditions. Most Aboriginal stories of creation tell about this sense of oneness and the relationships between the different beings inhabiting Earth.

Examples of creation stories that teach about this sense of oneness include the Rotinonshonni story of the earth evolving from an act of compassion by animals for a woman who fell from the sky world. Some animals gave up their lives by diving into the depths to find earth so woman had a place to live. In this first act of sacrifice, Aboriginal people learned they owed a sense of gratitude to the animals for providing the means to live on earth. One of the values that Aboriginal people gained from this act of creation was the value of reciprocation. The animals gave the means to sustain life and people reciprocated by showing their gratitude in specific ways. Today this gratitude is shown in hunting rituals and ceremonies followed after slaying an animal. Care is taken with the animal bones and prayers are offered prior to and after the killing. These practices maintain the connection between humans and the animals, preventing starvation. This story could be interpreted literally, allegorically or morally. With any deeply embedded cultural teaching, there is more than what is first seen. Creation stories are long and involved, resulting in the teaching of values in a complex manner that continues to provide invaluable lessons at each stage of ones life.

This is illustrated with the Rotinonshonni story of creation. The woman who fell from the sky had a daughter whose death provided the means for other forms of life. Her spirit enhanced the life-giving properties of the earth resulting in the beginning of plant life. Hence the earth is considered feminine, and since the sun's warmth results in life, it is considered the masculine component of the creative process. The sense of balance is maintained; the male/female component is interrelated, dependent on each for life, and held in balance.

Maintaining Balance through Reciprocity

Next in the story, the son of the departed daughter takes the earth from his mother's body, molds it into human form and blows on it, thus giving it life (Montour 1993). In return, the human being, upon passing from this order of existence at death, gives his body back to earth, restoring the life-giving properties to the Earth Mother who provides sustenance for plant life, people and animals. In this act of giving, human beings become part of the plant and animal kingdoms and the plants and animals become part of the human state. This continuous cycle of reciprocation exists between all forms of life in the world, held in balance and harmony through the reciprocal arrangements held between each life form.

While alive and inhabiting the world, Aboriginal people also help to ensure that the cycle continues through reciprocity, thereby keeping balance and harmony. This is done on a daily basis and at ceremonies held throughout the year. The Navaho refer to this maintenance of balance as *hozho* and the ceremony *hozhooi* (Blessingway). They, like many other Aboriginal peoples, believe that they have a responsibility to maintain *hozho*. Maintenance of harmony and balance can be done by reciting certain chants and prayers that help rejuvenate the earth. These also assist in preparing the way for the environment to replenish itself (Knudtson & Suzuki 1992). In addition to these ceremonial forms of replenishment, people use concrete forms such as planting beans with corn and squash. The Rotinonshonni for instance, planted corn, beans and squash together using a process called hill planting. Our people referred to these vegetables as *Teo ha ko* (Life Sustainers) and the three sisters. First three or four kernels of corn are placed into a hole and covered with soil. Two or three weeks later a few bean seeds are placed along the hill to provide nitrogen for the corn. The corn stalk provides a stem for the bean to climb. A squash or pumpkin seed is planted between the corn as ground cover to provide weed control for the beans and corn. This is another example of reciprocal arrangements among all forms of life (North East Indian Quarterly 1989).

Today, with the emphasis on technology many people have forgotten their connections with the earth and fail to recognize other forms of knowledge critical to our survival. Hunting cultures like the Beaver, a Dene people in the Northwest Territories, for instance, emphasize how to control their relationship with the rest of nature rather than how to control nature itself. This different mind set enables these people to be aware of and open to the forces and powers of the earth in ways that may not be available to those who overlook relatedness of all creatures. In addition, understanding the relationship with nature and how to utilize it requires a great deal of knowledge from all areas of wisdom, including spiritual and cognitive knowledge. When *Seeing the World with Aboriginal Eyes* the spiritual realm is of utmost importance for without knowledge in this area, the other knowledge is incomplete.

Maintaining the Ethic of Relatedness through Knowledge and Communities

The complexity of traditional knowledge is illustrated by Alcoze (1980) who said it takes superior knowledge to hunt with a bow and arrow than a gun. Hunting societies must have knowledge in many areas of science. Hunters must understand botany to select the best wood to make a bow; they must know anatomy to find sinew for a bow string; they must be skilled carpenters to carve the bow; they must understand aerodynamics to design an arrow that flies through the air; they must understand mathematics, algebra and statistics to plan the trajectory of an arrow in relation with the movement and distance of an animal; and they must understand zoology and ecology to follow an animal's movements. Regardless of all that needs to be known in the cognitive domain, the technical skills and academic knowledge, this is of little value without the spiritual beliefs, prayers, rituals and chants associated with hunting. The spiritual connection between the land and all its inhabitants is critical to well-being and survival.

In addition to hunting cultures, agriculturalists such as the Mayans also maintained this environmental philosophy by building their societies in harmony with the environment. Their complex cosmology, city plans, and homes reflected a deep connection between the earth world and sky world. Homes and communities conformed to the environment rather than conforming the environment to their homes (Bruchac 1993). Today in the ancient Mayan city of *Chichen Itza* elaborate temples are surrounded by freshly cut lawns and very few trees for the convenience of tourists; like many modern cities, this ancient city is devoid of wildlife. In contrast, walkways in the newly discovered Mayan village, *Coba,* are overshadowed by dense bush and trees. Traditionally, the Mayans built their homes and lived their lives with little effect on and in harmony with the environment, as did other traditional Aboriginal peoples. Today, many strive to return to this ethic by returning to their original traditions, rebuilding their relationships with other human and non-human beings; thereby reminding themselves of their responsibility to live in harmony with the natural world. For example, in Manitoba Aboriginal people are now planning their communities based on their own cultural understandings of relatedness to the earth, once again embracing the ethic of relatedness (Copet 1992). Doing this, the concept of relatedness becomes ever-present and envelopes the people at all times, thus making them continually aware of their spiritual connection with nature.

Maintaining the Ethic of Relatedness through Ceremonies
Some societies pattern their living arrangements on the ethic of relatedness while others maintain this ethic through ceremonies and rituals. For example, the Mayans no longer live in their ancient cities yet they retain their traditional philosophy and their ancestral ceremonies that reflect their connection with the environment. Corn provides the Mayans with physical nourishment and brings people into harmony with each other on a spiritual plane. There are complex cosmological implications involved in their relationship with corn which they maintain by thanking the spirits surrounding corn to ensure a good harvest and to reciprocate their connection to the cosmos. Participants

in these ceremonies are connected to its roots dating back to the Mayan creation story.

Ethic of the Environment

Today non-Aboriginal and Aboriginal people are becoming more conscious of environmental issues, particularly pollution and global warming, promoting the North American Aboriginal ethic of the environment as a way to care for and connect with the earth. Can only Aboriginal people adopt this ethic of the environment? Are non-Aboriginal people who adopt an Aboriginal philosophy appropriating something that is not theirs? Some believe that our salvation is dependent on others accepting this philosophy (Montour 1993). Snake (1993), a respected member of the Native American Church believes sharing his Lakota knowledge with non- Aboriginals will help develop a harmonious relationship between the two cultures, which is needed for both cultures to work together to protect the environment.

Promoting the Aboriginal ethic has increased the acceptance by the Euro-western scientific community of traditional environmental knowledge acquired by living in balance with Nature. Aboriginal communities now participate in environmental research. Collaborating with western-science researchers, elder's traditional environmental knowledge systems based on the ethic of relatedness and their extensive knowledge gained by living in close proximity with nature is now becoming an integral part of some scientific research. For example, the concept of sustainability used in ancient Dene traditions of the Northwest Territories is used to understand animal population statistics (Johnson 1992). In Northern Quebec, the Cree *nitibaaihitaan* (tallyman) is responsible for animal-related statistics. The *nitibaaihitaan* ensures safe harvests by setting beaver quotas and trapping dates to prevent trapping pregnant females. He also ensures trappers remain within their boundaries, informing him of new beaver lodges they might discover in neighbouring territories. Western scientists conducting this type of research require an understanding of wildlife movements and an acceptance of traditional environmental knowledge based on ancient beliefs and traditions as a valid form of knowledge.

The acceptance of Aboriginal knowledge on the part of the dominant cultures makes it possible for Aboriginal and Euro-western knowledge systems to work together to maintain a harmonious relationship between humans and the environment. Aboriginal people understand a Euro-western scientific method of evaluating environmental knowledge because our philosophy embodies scientific knowledge plus moral and spiritual realms of knowledge; however, Euro-western scientists find difficulties in incorporating Aboriginal philosophy with their science.

The sense of oneness that Aboriginal people have with Earth can be translated into a modern world but it must be remembered that the foundation is in the spiritual beliefs of the people: their ceremonies, rituals, teachings and stories that form the bedrock of their value system. To understand what it means to have this Aboriginal ethic one must search for the cosmological significance of Aboriginal beliefs. In this way, the patterns of thought that have been embedded within the schemata of Aboriginal peoples through their cultures are interpreted from the unique perspective of Aboriginal peoples.

RELATIONSHIPS WITH THE SPIRITS

The relationship between humans and our ancestor's spirits is explored in this section. The major theme is reincarnation and its relationship with relatedness, reciprocity, and maintaining balance in the world. The relatedness of humans to animals and humans to successive generations is pertinent to this discussion.

Aboriginal Understandings about Reincarnation

Reincarnation is often associated with Hinduism and Buddhism; many Aboriginal peoples have shared this belief for thousands of years (Mills 1992). How does this shamanic belief system affect the way that Aboriginal people interact with kin, their relationships with plants and animals, their well-being, and their connectedness to other people outside their own cultural group? [Note: 'Shamanic' refers generically to people who practice spirit relational ceremonies. Shamanism is a loaded term however a better term has yet to be identified.]

Each North American Aboriginal nation has their own beliefs concerning reincarnation, with some commonalities, and more prevalence of the belief with Aboriginal peoples living in the Arctic, Western Subarctic, and Northwest Coast (Mills 1994). For example, for Caribou Inuit in the Arctic, souls of the departed pass on to a feminine spirit residing in the sky where they are transformed and reborn on earth either as human beings or other forms of life (Knudston & Suzuki 1992). This reincarnated into animals or other beings illustrates the continuity and interrelatedness of life through an understanding of the cyclical nature of existence. Just as seasons are born and regenerated in the spring; through death, so do the spirits of the life forms on earth. As early as the sixteenth century, Jesuit missionaries recorded the

Algonquin and Huron peoples' belief in reincarnation, which was lost due to conversion to Christianity. Reincarnation remains an integral part of the world views of other societies, such as the Beaver and Gitskan (Mills 1988), perhaps because they were exposed to Christianity at a later date. Generally traditional Aboriginal peoples believe at death the soul is not extinguished and lives by investing another organism "with its sacred spark of vitality and consciousness" (Knudston & Suzuki: 41).

Like the eastern traditions, some Aboriginal people believe we are reincarnated because of the universal law of cause and effect and that parent's misdeeds are passed on to their children either during their lifetimes; or after death in future generations. This theme is prevalent in many Aboriginal cultures, for instance, pregnant women and their husbands follow specific behaviour patterns to prevent negatively affecting the child. One example of this is a hunter is loathe to kill when a new life is coming into his family, bringing the family near to hunger even though there is game nearby. The impact of an ancestor's inappropriate behaviour on future generations is found in many Aboriginal beliefs, such as the Gitksan (Mills 1988).

The belief that what you sow in this life is reaped in another is interpreted either literally or figuratively. Reincarnation is seen as a cycle of life and death that links the past, present and future, thereby strengthening ties to kin, land and the animals cohabiting on the land. This timeless view of life, with life being recreated in perpetuity through the souls of departed ones affects views on survival as a people and affects relationships with people in their immediate sphere.

Some Aboriginal people see the suffering of Aboriginal people and African descendants over the past centuries in North America by disease, slavery and loss of land as a direct result of cause and effect. At a colloquium at Morehouse College in Atlanta, Georgia on this subject, a question was posed which stirred great debate, particularly when an Inupiaq elder equated disease with accumulated karma for past misdeeds in other lives. To view reincarnation this way raises many serious and disturbing issues for Aboriginal people and others who have suffered in the colonization process. The debate became even more pronounced when discussing whether or not we are reincarnated into the same society in which we last lived. This raised serious concerns; for example, some people in the New Age Movement believe they were Aboriginal people in their past lives enabling them to appropriate Aboriginal ceremonies in their current life. This belief caused Aboriginal elders to be incensed with members of the New Age movement who commercialize Aboriginal spirituality for personal profit. Similar concerns are expressed with Aboriginal elders who have also commercialized Aboriginal spirituality. Concepts related to reincarnation are wrought with emotions and difficulties that cannot and will not readily disappear. The belief in reincarnation continues and since any viewpoint on the matter cannot be readily settled, perhaps it is best to set some of the more disturbing issues aside.

Three forms of reincarnation exist for Aboriginal peoples: the belief that souls from a deceased person can reincarnate into a newly born individual; the belief that animals can be reincarnated to help in the survival of humankind; and the belief that humans can be reincarnated into animal form and vice versa. There are variations such as multiple rebirths of the same individual within the same time span, which are included as a sub-topic in this discussion.

Numerous documented cases exist where people believe they or one of their relatives were reincarnated (Mills 1992). On a practical level, this can strengthen kinship ties. On a spiritual level, this form of reincarnation reinforces the belief of life continuing after death, and of the essence of a person remaining on earth to continue through the cycles of nature. The reincarnation of animals into future generations of their species could be seen as a practical and pragmatic belief that helps humankind survive. As long as the obligations and duties set out by the ethical, moral and spiritual beliefs of the people are followed or grievous consequences could result. Mills (1992: 17) states:

> [if] humans follow the ethics of human/animal interaction and treat these beings with respect and dispatch them so that they can find release in a spirit realm...they will choose to reincarnate, to give themselves once again to the sustenance of human beings.

Thus, it is crucial for those who take the life of a plant or an animal to consider not only their own well-being but those of future generations. In the third form where humans are reincarnated into other species, it illustrates that other life forms are viewed as close relatives, intimately linked with humans (Knudtson and Suzuki 1992). This perspective is more common to hunting societies. The outward appearance and behaviour of an animal as irrelevant to their relatedness to humans; the internal sacred spark of life unites all living things. Reincarnation is only one Aboriginal view on death, elaborate ceremonies ensure the passing of a person is simply a transition from one realm to the next. At the ceremonies of two important elders, the late Jacob Thomas

(Cayuga) and Art Solomon (Anishnawbe), the spirit departing rights exercised by those remaining in the earthly realm entailed watching over their spirits and helping them journey to the next realm. In Aboriginal cultures we remain participants with those that travel to the next realm, as they become participants with us who remain on this earth. Through four days of song, ceremony, feast and dance, Anishnawbe participants become healed within themselves and release the spirit of the departed so it can take the path to the spirit world with assurances that loved ones can continue on with their lives, in spite of their loss. The same occurs with the ten-day departing feast ceremony of the Rotinonshonni. In both traditions, after a year passes they bid their final farewell with a feast and by giving away the possessions of the departed. Thus they take the final steps of their own healing journey.

RELATIONSHIPS WITH THE SKY WORLD

This section examines the relationship that Aboriginal peoples have with the celestial bodies of the sky world. Themes include: 1) the earth world mirroring the celestial world; 2) the celestial world ordering the activities of the earth world; 3) the various cycles of life represented in the sky world; and 4) the commonalities that exist in the way many Aboriginal nations see their relationship with the sky world. Examples are drawn from a number of different Aboriginal nations in North America. The main focus of this section is to interpret relationships on physical, emotional, intellectual and spiritual levels (an Aboriginal interpretation) and on literal, anagogical, allegorical and moral/philosophical levels (a western interpretation).

Aboriginal Understandings of the Cosmos

Seeing the World with Aboriginal Eyes goes beyond the earthly realm. Aboriginal peoples' relationships exist within their cosmology of the natural world and of the celestial bodies. Stellar theology, called ethno-astronomy, is a fascinating way to understand a culture. However, in many areas of Aboriginal America, star knowledge is being forgotten due to changes occurring in the Aboriginal way of life. Knowledge once acquired by observers of the stars is now replaced by television, radio, film and the internet.

In years past, Aboriginal peoples utilized the sky to learn about the cosmos. They correlated celestial movements with their ways of life. Stars showed them when changes would take place in the environment. Although Aboriginal cultures had different cosmological explanations of the sky world, commonalities also existed. Aboriginal peoples organized their lives and their complex oral traditions around the movements of the stars. Their oral traditions included teachings and stories about the cosmology taught them the values, duties, obligations and responsibilities needed to live in balance and harmony with their culture and the universe. As a result, Aboriginal peoples adapted their cultures to the rhythmical movements of the stars. By studying the stars, they knew when to plant, hunt and move, for example, when to migrate from their winter to their summer grounds. From the stars they also developed societal laws and mores, and learned how to be a success as a human being. Knowledge on behaviour was also based on the stars, for example, courtship patterns were associated with the stars' movement.

Due to the directions and guidance received from the stars, Aboriginal people viewed the stars and other celestial bodies as sacred. In the winter, stories on how the stars came to be and why they appeared at certain times of the year were told. Stars personified the spirits of ancient ancestors who upon leaving this world left behind a spiritual imprint in the sky that Aboriginal societies could follow on earth. Among the Anishnawbe, two of these spirits seen in the stars are *Nanabush* and *Shingabus.* Other Aboriginal peoples have their own traditional heroes represented in the stars. As each constellation appears in the night sky, stories are about the adventures of the traditional heroes. It takes up to four days to recite the teachings of one constellation.

One of the most knowledgeable Anishnawbe authorities on celestial knowledge is the late Dan Pine from the Garden River reserve near Sault Ste. Marie. Dan Pine learned celestial knowledge from a traditional elder named *Wabmaymay*, a member of the *Wabeno* (Dawn Light Society) (Williamson and Farrer 1992). The *Wabeno* study the heliacal rise and setting of star constellations. The term "heliacal" refers to the first and last time a star group is seen in the night sky in correlation with the sun's path. Like the sun, stars travel clockwise from east to west, however at certain times of the year some constellations are only seen in the night sky. When a constellation appears in the night sky the *Wabeno* inform the community what ceremonies should take place, thereby setting the rhythms of daily and seasonal living.

In addition to watching the stars, Aboriginal people such as the Lakota study the position of the sun in relation to the star constellations. Their ceremonial Sundance is conducted at the summer solstice when the power of the sun is strongest and the days are longest. The Lakota also see the earth world as a mirror of the celestial world, setting up ceremonies and migrations in accordance to the heliacal rising and setting of star groups, and the occurrences of equinoxes and solstices.

Each constellation or celestial event corresponds with Lakota ceremonial centres such as Red Clay Valley encircling the Black Hills (Goodman 1992).

Thomas (1997) told a story that during the month of October, the Rotinonshonni looked to the sky and when the constellation Ursa Major (Big Dipper) reached a certain point hunting season began. In the story, the hunters hold a bow, a knife and a kettle and are bear hunting. They are represented as the three stars outlining the handle of the dipper; the four stars outlining the scoop of the dipper are the bear. When the constellation reaches the most northerly point in the heliacal rise and is directly above the Rotinonshonni, the hunters have a shot at the bear. Autumn then begins with the leaves turning red from the blood of the bear and the hunting season starts. The heliacal setting of the Pleiades, another cluster of seven stars, signified the end of hunting and the beginning of growing or birthing season. The Rotinonshonni story about the Pleiades tells of seven brothers who go hungry and are raised into the air becoming stars (Parker 1989). The time of planting, when the Pleiades set is the lean period. People look forward to the rising of the Pleiades in August signifying the beginning of the fall harvest (Foster 1974). The Pleiades (called the 'Bear's Head') are also significant to the Anishnawbe. When these stars rose above the Stern Paddler (called 'Orion's Belt') in the night sky, the *Wabeno* knew it was time for the Anishnawbe to begin moving to their summer villages. Therefore, when the Pleiades was above Orion's Belt, or as the Anishnawbe say, when the Bear's Head was above the Stern Paddler, it signified that the bear had left her lair to look for a mate (Jiles 1995). The Northern Anishnawbe followed suit. The young people of marriageable age would begin looking for a spouse and begin courting.

Aboriginal peoples' understanding of the world is directly related to their understanding of the stars. For the Northern Anishnawbe, the Polar Star or North Star, known as the Bow Paddler keeps the canoe steady. When fall arrives, three other stars appear in the night sky and are known as Stern Paddler or Orion's Belt. The Stern Paddler steers the canoe and sets the cosmos in motion. Stern Paddler appears from November to early April bringing the winter season in and out as he steers the canoe throughout the cosmos (Jiles 1995). Traditionally, the Northern Anishnawbe divided their universe between the Bow Paddler and the Stern Paddler. The Bow Paddler remains stationary in the northern hemisphere and has been used as a beacon and guide for centuries. The Rotinonshonni tell a story about Star Boy leading a lost band of hunters back home, guided by the Polar or North Star. For the Lakota, each of the eleven sacred sites visited annually correlate with a constellation.

The sun travels through each of these constellations; Lakota follow the sun's path and when it enters a specific constellation they perform the related ceremony at the associated sacred site. One reason for following the stars, moon and sun is to be a participant in the circle of life, thereby helping to maintain the balance of life. The rhythmical nature to life on earth is set by the celestial bodies. The Lakota follow this rhythm in their daily activities and spiritual ceremonies.

Another important component of celestial knowledge is the moon calendar used by most Aboriginal people. For the Caribou Inuit the moon defines the year's stages (Knudtson & Suzuki 1992) and their calculations of the seasons. The Lakota followed a moon calendar to help guide them in their migrations. The Rotinonshonni followed a moon calendar based on a twenty-eight day month with thirteen moon months to the year, which is ten days short of the solar year. They added an extra moon every third year to stay in harmony with the solar year. The traditional Anishnawbe moon calendar is described by the Ojibwe Cultural Foundation (1990) and has become in tune with the one used by mainstream society:

January	*Mnidoo-Giizis*	Spirit Moon
February	*Mkwa-Giizis*	Bear Moon
March	*Naabdin-Giizis*	Snowcrust Moon
April	*Booboogame-Giizis*	Broken Snowshoe Moon
May	*Nmedine-Giizis*	Sucker Moon
June	*Waabgonii-Giizis*	Blooming Moon
July	*Miin-Giizis*	Berry Moon
August	*Mnoomni-Giizis*	Wild Rice Moon
September	*Waabbagaa-Giizis*	Harvest Moon
October	*Bnaakwii-Giizis*	Falling Leaves Moon
November	*Baaskkaakodin-Giizis*	Freezing Moon
December	*Mnidoo-Giisoonhs*	Little Spirit Moon

Names for months vary geographically, for example, where corn is grown a month is named for when the corn ripens, in another area the month might be named after the ripening of strawberries or blackberries. The main point is that the Anishnawbe and other Aboriginal peoples' calendars are based on the cycles of nature, with the moon as the defining element, illustrating our connection with the sky world. In this way, the earth world reflects what is happening in the sky world.

Larger more sedentary Aboriginal societies such as the Aztec and Mayans also based their complex calendars on the movement of the moon as well as the planets, stars and sun. They knew that every 52 years the nine planets lined up in order and they built ceremonial centres in line with their movements. These centres contained information about the sun, moon and stars.

The Mayans spent a great amount of time looking at the movements of celestial bodies and built their cities as miniature representations of the cosmos. Unlike small northern societies that moved to different parts of their territory in a cycle defined by the celestial bodies, the Mayans were sedentary yet their daily existence was also defined by the cycles of the stars. Structures, such as *Chichen Itza*, were built so that they lined up with the equinoxes and solstices. Other buildings also served as observatories (Tompkins 1976), keeping the people informed when certain constellations, planets, and the sun and moon were in specific locations. Their complex cosmology was intertwined with the physical movements of the universe, giving order and meaning to their lives. For example, the pyramid at *Chichen Itza* seen when looking at the Great Temple was a time calculating devise based on ancient Mayan calendars (Humbatzmen 1990). It is a square pointing to the four directions and four seasons with 91 steps, each representing a season, on each side of the square. Four multiplied by 91 represents 364 days of the year with the five remaining quarters symbolized on top of the pyramid. Finally, every 52 years during the summer solstice, a shadow of a snake made by the sun appears and climbs up the side of the steps representing change and renewal in the 52 year Mayan calendar cycle. At this time all nine known planets are in alignment.

At *Teotihuacan* Mexico, where a civilization similar to the Aztec and Mayans resided and created large ceremonial temple structures, engineer Hugh Harleston Jr. found the city plan was based on measurements correlated with the Earth's circumference. Other measurements confirmed the city was a scale model of Earth and our solar system, including distances to all nine planets and their orbits around the sun. Included in his findings was a planet twice as far as Pluto from the sun. It will be interesting to see if this planet is discovered by future scientists (Tompkins 1976).

Other less sedentary northern Aboriginal Societies also built ceremonial centres where they calculated the movement of the sun, moon and stars, such as the medicine wheel at Big Horn, Montana. This medicine wheel has a 28 day lunar cycle aligned with the solstice sunrise, sunset, and the star constellations appearing in the morning of the solstice. The star Rigel appears 28 days after the solstice and then Sirius appears telling the people it is time to leave the mountains. These structures are found throughout the prairies and are analog computers, which are non-electrical devices mimicking phenomena in order to record observations and measurements of phenomena. Aboriginal peoples on the prairies used this to locate the position of the stars so they conducted their ceremonies in alignment with the summer and winter solstice (Giese1996).

Much can be learned from a nation's understanding of the stars, including: how they order their lives, when they have their ceremonies, how they perceive their responsibilities and obligations in life, how they adapt their lives to the cyclical movements of celestial bodies, and what values form the foundation of their belief system. Food habits, hunting practices, planting and harvesting of crops, collecting medicines, and courtship patterns, are only a few details of everyday life found in the celestial bodies. Even though there are diverse Aboriginal nations throughout North America, each with their own oral traditions about the cosmos, they share commonalities in their interpretations of the movements of the celestial bodies. Therefore, *Seeing the World with Aboriginal Eyes* is related to ones star knowledge.

Chapter Three

WESTERN DOOR:
COMING TO KNOWING

Aboriginal cultures have ways through which the Ancient Spirits and Powers of the cosmos speak to and help people in times of great suffering, dreams and visions are a personal way, a hero-restorer is a more public means. *Nanabush* of the Anishnawbe, Sweet Medicine of the Cheyenne and *Tekanawitah* of the Rotinonshonni are a few examples of hero-restorers, figures who re-establish balance within the lives of community members. People learn how to lead a good life from hero-restorers. In this section, an examination of the Rotinonshonni Great Law of Peace that came about through the efforts of *Tekanawitah*, the *Peacemaker*, are investigated. This provides insights into social order, world view and ethos of the Rotinonshonni, as well as insights into the teachings of the *Peacemaker* that embody a unique way to see the world.

The Birth of the Hero/Restorer

When Aboriginal societies suffer from social breakdown, the values in their society are sometimes restored by the coming of a person who restores both the cosmic and social order of balance in that society. Both past and present cultural figures perform this task and these figures are referred to as a hero/restorer in western discourse, reflecting the monumental task of transforming society in difficult times. According to Campbell (1988: 123), a non-Aboriginal instructor who taught about the mythical heroes of both traditional and ancient societies, a hero is:

> ...someone who does something beyond the
> normal range of achievement and experience
> [and]... someone who has given his or her
> life to something bigger than oneself.

Heroes are defined as able to experience the supernatural by accessing the spiritual realm. A psychological transformation occurs within the person and they are reborn, giving their life over to the lives of others. Heroes are also defined as those who accomplish something grand for humanity's sake, sacrificing oneself for other people or an idea.

This sacrifice of the self is the ultimate form of compassion or love of humankind. It is represents acceptance of a higher ideal.

Often, the hero goes on a spiritual quest. Through knowledge of his/her quest, people appreciate the capabilities and potentialities of humankind. Physical courage, compassion, sacrifice, wisdom and love for all form a basis for the heroic act. These values give voice to deeper longings dormant in people through the outward manifestation of the hero's actions. It is necessary for a healthy society to give of oneself to achieve something worthwhile, societies need heroes to remain healthy.

Heroes are sensitive to the needs of his/her times (Campbell 1988) and out of the hero's life comes a new way of being or behaving. The founding of a new age, a way of life or a cultural tradition could be the result of a hero's actions. The hero shows humankind how to develop their own humanity, how to care for others, how to live by the values that form the cultural basis of society, how to access the powers to transform one's life, how to release oneself from fear to live a life of harmony, and how to confront the suffering in life thereby releasing others from suffering. A hero also performs acts that go beyond his/her own death, acts that benefit and transform society into a better place to live.

For the Rotinonshonni, heroes epitomize values embedded in their cosmology and inner conscience. These values help the society remain in balance and are based on the stories of their cosmology such as the creation story. Social reform has occurred several times, resulting in restoring balance through acts of social reformers or heroes. These social reformers/heroes renew elements of their cosmology to fit contemporary conditions. The first hero to achieve this was the *Peacemaker* who created the Rotinonshonni Confederacy. There are many members of the Rotinonshonni who presently wait for a new hero to arrive.

The Story of the *Peacemaker*

This is an abbreviated version of the story originally told to me by Thomas (1997). Traditions formulated from this story are known as *Kayeneren: kowa* (Great Law of Peace). The *Peacemaker* arrived when nations, who later became the Rotinonshonni Confederacy, were fighting amongst one another. The Creator was saddened by what his children in the earth world were doing to each other; they were living in a continual cycle of violence. The Creator knew he had to restore harmony so he sent a messenger who based his teachings on elements in the Rotinonshonni story of creation.

The sky world was above the earth world, it was where the keeper of the earth and the owner of the Tree of Light existed. At the centre of the sky world rested a Great Pine Tree. On top of the tree perched *Agatoni heno* who promised to aid his nephew and niece if they ever needed help. *Agatoni heno* is also represented as the Great Dew Eagle who watches over his children and as the Great Reverence. To reach this tree the beings of the sky world went through an initiation process. Only two children had the ability to make it. The female child with the help of her brother and after many trials and tests; finally made it up to the top of the Tree. She was told by her uncle, *Agatoni heno*, she would marry the owner of the Tree of Light, and through her blossoms restore light to the sky world. After many trials and tests, she arrived and married the owner of the Tree of Light who oversaw the inhabitants of the sky world. One day she and the owner of the Tree of Light sat at the edge of a chasm at the base of the Tree of Light. In a fit of jealousy, the owner of the tree pushed her through the chasm. As she burst through the womb of the sky, she fell to the world below, beginning life in the world below and dimming light in the sky world above. The light from the tree had slowly gone dim; the owner's wife through her blossoms brought new light to the sky world. This light brought a new beginning to the world below. The light in the sky world was extinguished until her grandson *Teharonhia:wako* rekindled it by setting the sun, moon, and stars in motion in the sky.

As the owner of the Tree of Light's wife fell, the waterfowl who are the first order of creation because of their ability to fly, swim and live on land, and the first being thrown from the sky world, saw her coming and rose up to cushion her landing. Next, the beaver, otter and muskrat dove deep into the water and the muskrat retrieved some earth for the woman to rest on, dying as he reached the surface. The beaver and otter took the earth from muskrats paw and placed it on the back of a turtle and the waterfowl lowered the woman onto it.

Not long after coming to rest on the turtle, the woman had a daughter from the Great Turtle Man who supported her after her fall. Their daughter, Blooming Flowers, bore two sons *Teharonhia:wako* and *Sawiskera*. Each affected the world. *Sawiskera* (Ice Like Flint) burst through the side of his mother killing her with his power to freeze. *Teharonhia;wako* (He Who Holds The Heavens) always looked to the sky for the answers needed to renew his mothers life. These sons created all things in the world, including the *onkwe honwe* human beings. Everything *Teharonhia:wako* created in perfect balance, *Sawiskera* created something to disrupt the balance. After defeating his brother in a contest, *Teharonhia:wako* divided Turtle Island. He sent his brother to live across the Great Water and eventually into the deepest recesses of the sky world. *Sawiskera* returns every year augmented by the night sky and the north wind to try to gain control of creation; however, he has limited power. Later, some of the *onkwe honwe* flourished, migrating up a great river, now known as the Mississippi, following one of its tributaries, which they called Ohio meaning beautiful river. They arrived in a territory of five lakes, formed like the fingers on a hand created when *Teharonhia:wako* scratched the earth, settling to live in peaceful co-existence with each other for a time.

As the years went by, the people became divided into five different nations: *Kenienké: haka* (Mohawk), *Oneota: haka* (Oneida), *Onontaka:haka* (Ononta:ka), *Kaokwa:haka* (Cayuga) and the *Sonontowa:haka* (Seneca). They began to dispute until warfare finally erupted between them, soon spreading to other nations. Some nations, including the Wendat (Hurons), moved north because warfare destroyed their harmony of life.

Within the Wendat nation lived a woman and her daughter. She feared her daughter would be killed in the warfare and decided to move to a place where she could safely raise her daughter. She settled on a bay at the eastern shores of a great lake whose waters flowed into a river that went to an ocean. When her daughter reached the age of womanhood, she was placed in seclusion. Traditionally this was called putting her under the husk, like a secluded husk of corn, and prepared her for adulthood. Not long after coming out of seclusion, her mother noticed her daughter looked pregnant and a few months later she gave birth to a male child. This distressed the grandmother. She berated her daughter and her new grandchild. She even tried to take his life on several occasions.

One evening, while the child's grandmother was resting, a visitor appeared in the dark. He told her not to be angry with her daughter and her grandson. He told her the boy was born to bring a message to the people, which would restore order in the society and beyond. The boy's grandmother had feared the child might have been *otkon* (imbalanced) because of his unnatural birth, but now she knew that he was special and had a purpose that would benefit humankind. The next day, she looked out of her lodge and saw the tracks of a rabbit. The great light being often took the form of a rabbit when it appeared on the earth.

As the boy grew older the grandmother brought him and her daughter back to their Wendat village to visit his relatives. It was not long after that he began to do the work that had been prophesied for him. The Wendat children were trained in the art of warfare at a young age. The young *Peacemaker* seeing what they were learning told them to stop and listen. He told them to put away their weapons and to work towards peace. From peace, they could start once again to live in a righteous manner. Once all of them joined together in this way of living, they would have a power they had never known before. It would come from having a good mind and righteous living resulting in peace. The elders overheard the young man and called a meeting to discuss what the boy was teaching. Shortly after the Wendat warriors put their weapons away for good, for the war chief said, "How is it that a young boy could be so wise and we adults be so childish." In this way, warfare ended in the Wendat territory. For peace to last the young *Peacemaker* still had work to do as they needed a system to unite them in peace.

After bringing peace to the Wendat, the young man and his family moved back to the bay by the lake where he had been born. Not long after, he told his grandmother and mother it was time for him to continue his work, for there were still warring nations further south that needed to be healed. He cut into a nearby oak tree and as the tree bled its sap, the young *Peacemaker* told his mother and grandmother that this tree will live a very long time. If you see the sap turn red like blood something has happened to me. He then crossed the Great Lake in a stone white canoe and paddled to the south side where he came to a trail. It was also in a stone white canoe that the *onkwe honwe* make their spiritual journeys in this realm and the other realms of existence.

As the young *Peacemaker* landed on the shore of the lake, a Kenienké man named *Torewatario* (He Does Everything Right), saw him coming, greeted him and warned him he would be in danger. The *Peacemaker* replied, "They are the ones I am looking for." He then said "*Torewatar:io* go tell the *Kenienké: haka* warchiefs, I am coming." As the *Peacemaker* traveled to the west of the southern side of the great lake there resided a cannibal who ate the hearts of the warriors he killed to gain their *orenta*. The *Peacemaker* climbed to the top of the cannibal's lodge and looked down through a smoke hole into a cooking vessel. The cannibal upon seeing the beautiful reflection in the water became remorseful for his actions. The *Peacemaker* climbed down and told the cannibal, "From now on the selected men will have a good mind, and shall wear the antlers of the deer on their heads. Like I am showing you, they will feast on the meat of the deer and like the buck deer watch over their people."

After traveling some more he met a woman named *Jokansasee* (Face Like a Cat) who lived on the great war trail and fed the warriors as they passed through on their way to battle. The *Peacemaker* told the woman,

"It is time to quit feeding the warriors because there is a greater work for her to do. From the time of creation it was a woman who restored life to the world. The women are the agents of creation.... From now on, the women will be paramount in making decisions about war and peace because they are the life bringers. Whenever the male leaders come together to speak, they will be subject to the will of the women who will have the consensus of the community. The women will choose the leaders from the men. It's the men's duty to uphold the peace and the women will depose any leaders who forfeit their duty."

The *Peacemaker* then traveled eastward through all of the villages along the way, until he came to the falls where two great rivers divided and two *Kenienké: haka* warriors met him. They brought him to their great warchief and two sub warchiefs. One of the sub warchiefs had heard about the *Peacemaker*, from *Torewater:io* and had waited a long time for this moment. The great warchief said to the *Peacemaker*, "If you can pass a test, we will accept your message of peace." They brought the *Peacemaker* to a tree overlooking the embankment and told him climb on a branch overlooking the river. They then cut the branch and the *Peacemaker* plunged into the river. The next day, the two warriors saw the smoke of a fire. When they went to investigate, the *Peacemaker* was sitting by the fire. They brought him back to the village and the warchief accepted the message of peace, righteous living, and the power that comes from having a good mind. He then gave the three warchiefs titles that would be passed on forever: *Takarihoken* (His Mind Was Divided), *Ayenwatha* (He Stayed Awake), and *Shatekariwate* (Two Things Equal). The *Peacemaker* relied on *Ayenwatha*, to help pass on his message.

"If anyone was burdened with grief, I would console him by taking the skin of a fawn and wiping his eyes."

"I would talk to the person and clear their ears and help them listen again. I would clear the obstructions from their throat so that they could speak clearly once again." Each time the Peacemaker spoke, *Ayenwatha* felt a bit better. He continued, "When someone is grieving, I will give them *onanora* medicine, and relieve their stomach. I would wipe away any blood stains so that no one would remember the pain. I would lift the covering of darkness with these kind words. I would clear the view to the sky so that they could see its beauty. I would raze up the sun so that when they turned the shadow will be behind them rather than in front. I would cover the grave of the dead person with elm bark so as not to let the sun or the rain in. I would bind the bones of the departed with wampum and relay twenty matters of sympathy. I would have the faith keepers gather the logs and relight the fire. I would make sure the clan mother looks after the *Royaner* (Good Minded) and that his seat is always filled and his seat never goes cold. When someone is in grief, they will stay away from certain plants in the swamp, they can harm themselves with."

Then the *Peacemaker* finished by saying, "Just as I have done to you, when a *Royaner* departs, those from the other side of the fire will be notified and they will come to console the loss. You always need two people to comfort one another.

Once *Ayenwatha* was consoled, he was ready to work with the *Peacemaker* in bringing peace to the other nations. They traveled west and *Ayenwatha* stopped where an *Oneota:haka* man was guarding the corn fields. He stayed that evening, and that evening the *Peacemaker* arrived. The guardian of the cornfield traveled to the great warchief explaining what had happened. The warchief asked for a sign before the *Peacemaker* and Ayenwatha entered the village. The *Peacemaker* gave him a beaded eagle feather and told him the message of peace, power and righteousness that comes from having a good mind. He then gave the three chiefs their titles *Rotatshe:the* (Quiver Bearer), *Kanonkwenio:ton* (He Gathers The Corn), and *Teiohakwente* (He looks Through The Opening).

Two nations accepted the peace, and the *Peacemaker* said to them, "We will bypass the next nation until we are stronger and come back to them later." They walked westward until they passed the *Onontaka:haka* country and ended by the lake where the *Kaokwa:haka* lived. The *Kaokwa:haka* had already heard about the great peace that was taking place and so accepted the message of the *Peacemaker*. Because there were two main *Kaokwa:haka* villages, the *Peacemaker* gave a

title of "Goodminded" to the warchief of the lower lake *Kaokwa:haka,
Takaenionk* (He Looks Both Ways) and then to the warchief of the upper
lake, *Katsinontawehon* (On His Knees).

They then traveled to the country of the powerful *Sonontowa:
haka* where they could only get two warchiefs to agree to the great peace.
The *Peacemaker*, gave them their titles, *Skaniatar:io* (Beautiful Lake)
and *Shatekaron:ies* (He Looks To The Sky). The *Peacemaker* said that
after we convince the *Onontaka:haka* at their village *Kanata:kowa,* we
will send for the other two warchiefs that did not accept the message.
It was at that time *Jokansasee* arrived. Together, the *Peacemaker,
Ayenwatha, Jokansasee* and a contingent from each of the nations
traveled back to the lake where the Onontaka: haka lived, headed by the
great warchief *Tatotaho* (The Entangled). After crossing the lake they
were confronted by *Tatotaho* and all of his warriors. The four nations
surrounded *Tatotaho.* With the kind words of *Jakonsasee, Ayenwatha*
combed the tangles from his hair. The *Peacemaker* said to *Tatotaho,*
"You will be without a mother, and from now on be known as a bearer
of names if you accept the peace we offer here." *Tatotaho* replied, "I
will accept the peace on the condition that *Kanata:kowa* becomes a
place where we will gather and come to resolutions to keep the peace."
The *Peacemaker* agreed and sang a song of peace. Finally, he sent for
the two *Sonontowa:haka* warchiefs who had not yet accepted the peace.
They agreed to join the great peace if they were allowed to be the door
keepers for anyone who wanted to enter the territory of the Longhouse.
The *Peacemaker* agreed. While at *Onontaka,* the *Peacemaker* said to
everyone,

> "This is the place where we will plant a tree to
> represent the peace that all of us would live under. The
> tree's branches will shade and protect the people and
> on top of the tree would sit an eagle who would watch
> over us….Uproot the tree and throw the weapons into
> a chasm that formed. Let new life be born. In this way,
> the weapons would be gone forever."

Then *Jakonsasee* and the mothers of the nations placed antlers on those
they deemed worthy of the *Keyeneren Kowa* (Great Peace) making 50
Royaner in all. The *Peacemaker* restored the balance that had existed
in the sky world, by recreating the Rotinonshonni cosmology in the
earth world. Many years later another reformer named *Skaniatar:io*
(Handsome Lake) renewed this process when the Rotinonshonni
lost access to much of their territory. *Skaniatar:io* condensed the

Rotinonshonni cosmology originally created by the *Peacemaker* to fit in the territory of the five nations, so it fit into what had formally been a place of residence, the Longhouse, creating the Longhouse Tradition existing today.

Learning about the feats of *Takanawitah* and *Skaniatar:io*, we can learn how the acts of these two men accomplished the work of heroes – restoring the world to balance and harmony, teaching the importance of compassion, sharing, giving and sacrifice, and illustrating how, from the hero's life, renewal comes to a nation and her people. In essence, the hero shows the people the path to follow so that the people can live their lives in accordance to the principles of the Creator and the universal laws of humankind. The role of the *Peacemaker* is found throughout Native America. This hero/restorer figure is found historically and in oral tradition. It arouses the desire to follow the righteous path in life or the "Red Road."

MODERN QUEST FOR WISDOM AND THE SACRED

This section shares the life and teachings of Jacob Thomas, Rotinonshonni Chief, *Teononwithon* (Two Events). In these teachings more of the Rotinonshonni world view, cosmology, ways of knowing and life ways are presented. Most importantly, these teachings offer a rationale for existence and a method to achieve peace, power, and righteousness through appreciation, love, respect and generosity. Thus, *The Kari:wio* (Good Message), brought to *Skaniatar:io* and the *Keyeneren Kowa* (Great Law of Peace) are traditions that Jacob Thomas was renowned for and are important components of tradition for many members of the Rotinonshonni Confederacy. Modern dilemmas face the Aboriginal nations in North America and these teachings address many of these concerns. The applicability of the teachings to modern times and the difficulties that are faced in maintaining the *Kari:wio* are also described. What can be gained from the teachings, which is of great significance, is the knowledge of the morals and ethics underscoring the philosophy of life of the Rotinonshonni people and their search for meaning and union with the Creator through the establishment of codes of behaviour.

Aboriginal Societal Understandings of Codes and Behaviour

Every society has morals, ethics, mores and laws of behaviour that form the ethical and moral foundation of that society. Stripping away the cultural framework, the many core values or ethos underscoring the beliefs and daily practices of a society can be determined. Through the daily practice of these values a connection with the Sacred is attained. Such values as sharing, wisdom, respect, love, humility, kindness, and courage are common to many peoples but each North American Aboriginal person's perspective on these values and way of practicing these values are culturally unique.

In modern and historical times people have sought to follow a path that offers peace within themselves and a meaning for their existence; many Aboriginal peoples call this path the Red Road. For some people, such as the Anishnawbe, it is called the search for *pimadaziwin*. For the Rotinonshonni, it is called following the Teachings From The Longhouse, including the Code of Handsome Lake *Kari:wio* (Good Message)(Thomas and Boyle 1994). Gaining an insight into Jacobs Thomas' life helps one begin to know and understand the philosophical underpinnings of Rotinonshonni thought and life ways. We can also learn of the struggles that face those who wish to live a traditional life that may be at odds with the lifestyles promoted in the modern world by the dominant cultures. The life of Thomas is portrayed along with the issues that face him as both a traditional leader and faith keeper in his struggle to maintain and promote the traditional belief system of his people and their philosophy of life.

Chief Jacob Thomas was brought up during a time when there were few conveniences, and no quick means of transportation or communication. Society was transitioning from traditional to modern times. Thomas adapted to changes taking place in his own society as well as those of other people. In spite of these changes, he retained his traditional core values. For fourteen years, he successfully taught Rotinonshonni culture and language at Trent University, imparting the knowledge acquired as a youth living on the Six Nations Reserve near Brantford, Ontario.

When Jacob Thomas was a boy, his father David Thomas was a traditional chief and ceremonialist. His father, a gifted orator, recited both the *Kayeneren Kowa* (Great Law of Peace) and *Kari:wio* (Good Message), known as the Code of Handsome Lake. Along with the creation story, these teachings were the foundation of the Rotinonshonni oral tradition. Chief Thomas sat for hours listening to his father, watching him practice the ceremonies and recite the sacred traditions. Elders from the different Rotinonshonni communities visited Chief Thomas' father, staying for months. In this way, Jacob Thomas accumulated knowledge from the different traditions.

Thomas believed his accomplishments are much harder to achieve today. The youth of today are less attentive due to the influence of television, radio, movie theatres and other media. When Thomas was young, reciting stories about the Rotinonshonni culture was a means of learning and also entertainment. Today, youth are less inclined to follow the same practices and share the same values as their ancestors due to changes in lifestyle and family structure. Today the nuclear family is the predominant; in the past the common family unit was the extended clan. Today many Rotinonshonni young people no longer know what clan they belong to, making it difficult for them to identify with their ancestral traditions. However, Thomas believed the Rotinonshonni wisdom, values and spirituality still benefit contemporary youth. This was reinforced by his experience teaching at the university. When he spoke about the *Kayeneren: kowa* or the *Kari:wio*, two other parts of the oral tradition of the Rotinonshonni that impart their ethos, world view and life ways, many students said how the teachings transformed their lives, indicating these teachings are as relevant today as they were in the past. In addition, Thomas and his wife took a group of us and some elders to the state of New York, visiting places mentioned in the oral tradition of the Great Law. The final resting place of *Skaniatar:io* , who received the teachings of the *Kari:wio*, was also on the itinerary. A few non-Aboriginal people joined the group and when the journey was over one of the non-Aboriginal participants reported things he learned on the trip would change the way he led the rest of his life.

Traditional teachings form the foundation on which culture is built. How members relate to one another, how they relate to other life forms and how they practice their traditions are only a few ways that these teachings impact the lives of a people. Thomas taught that the core values of the culture are found within the creation story of the Rotinonshonni. Unity is taught at the first part of the Creation story, when the mother was killed by one of her sons and her spirit entered the earth and became Earth Mother giving life to plants, other life forms, and human beings. This teaches that a unity exists between every different living thing and that human beings emulate the actions of the Earth Mother at the time of their death. When a person dies, the body re-enters the Earth Mother offering life to the other forms of creation.

Many years after the time of creation, the Five Nations who would make up the Rotinonshonni Confederacy, began to war and a prophet named *Peacemaker* restored harmony resulting in a Confederacy based on principles of peace. These principles of peace became know as the *Kayeneren:kowa* or the Great Law of Peace. The Great Law informs the Rotinonshonni, even to this day, on how to live without strife among each and other nations. Many years later after the American War of Independence, when once again the Rotinonshonni began to fight amongst each other, messengers from the spirit world were sent to a traditional chief of the Seneca, *Skaniatar:io* (Handsome Lake) who taught him a moral code applied by Rotinonshonni members to their personal lives. This code taught Rotinonshonni members they would have to live under these rules if they were to continue to exist as a society. The Rotinonshonni refer to this Code as the *Kari:wio* (Good Message). This Code set the stage for the Rotinonshonni to continue their existence as a nation into a modern age.

These prophets, the *Peacemaker* and Handsome Lake, came in times of strife to help their people. Thomas believed that the Rotinonshonni are once again living under trying times and if the young people continue to deviate from the traditional Rotinonshonni culture and values established in the Code, the Rotinonshonni nation will end. Part of the *Kari:wio* proclaims that failing to follow this Code places the Rotinonshonni nation and the world in danger. The Code says it is up to human beings to reform their way of living if they want the world to continue to exist. The *Kari:wio*, although set down many years before modern inventions and industry, mentions future problems with pollution, modern warfare, in vitro fertilization and abortion. All these are mentioned as part of the breakdown of society that Rotinonshonni members will face in their lives. Most importantly, the Code is a path that the Rotinonshonni should follow through life. The teachings are imparted through recitations every year in the Longhouse and contain morals, ethics and prophecies of the future, as well as lists of punishments for those who have not followed the Good Message.

The Code is not accepted by all Rotinonshonni traditionalists, because some believe it is influenced by Christian teachings. Others believe the Code stands alone and is a continuation of the values found in the creation story and the Great Law of Peace. Nonetheless, the Code of Handsome Lake can be considered as the catalyst which helped preserve Rotinonshonni culture during the people's most trying times. *Skaniatar:io* amalgamated many of the traditional teachings that preceded the Code, such as the cycle of ceremonies in the Longhouse.

Many Aboriginal university students have little traditional knowledge of their culture. Traditionalists believe it is time that the culture finds new venues for expression; the university is one such setting, although there is controversy over what should be taught. For teachers like Chief Jacob Thomas there are a number of reasons to bring the teachings of Aboriginal cultures into a more open venue of learning. The people who belong to a traditional culture and those who do not have a common need for the values and truths taught in these teachings. Consequently, elders believe if the teachings are restricted only to cultural members and the prophecies are true, then there is little hope for change in the world. The dominant society brought the greatest changes to the world; if they are left out there is little chance for a change for the better. The Rotinonshonni traditional teachers restrict the most sacred parts of their traditions, which are culturally exclusive to their own cultural members. In this way, they cannot be accused of minimizing or even desecrating the sacredness of their traditions yet share teachings needed to address prophesies.

In conclusion, these traditional teachers believe we are living in a time when the teachings are needed the most, especially among the young with little moral direction in their lives. Traditional teachers offer an alternative understanding on how we may live in a world based on a different cultural world view.

THE NECESSITY OF SACRIFICE

Sacrifice is a cherished part and a recurrent theme throughout many Aboriginal cultures. In fact, its repetition indicates that it is a necessary part to one's existence if one is to live a full and rich life. Consequently, as a part of their spiritual orientation, many Aboriginal people make sacrifices to the Creator and other spiritual forces, giving up precious objects or part of their being as gifts to others (to both human, other – than – human people and the Creator) in the hope that goodwill result from the sacrifice either to themselves, others or their nation. For instance, the Dakota in the Sundance ceremony give of themselves, thus strengthening the sacred hoop of their nation. It is this tradition that I was exposed to and participated in during my time in western Canada. Numerous other examples can be found throughout Aboriginal North America. Therefore, this section will examine the occurrence of this mind set and explore the underlying rationale for it through an examination of the Sundance and the practice of giveaways.

The Meaning of Sacrifice

Part of the mind set of *Seeing the World with Aboriginal Eyes* is the idea that people need to make sacrifices throughout their lives.

This may include making an offering or saying prayers as part of the ceremonial life of the people, but often it requires making an offering of a most valuable possession to the Creator or others. For instance, among the Dakota, there is nothing that is more valuable than the offering of a piece of oneself to the Creator; in other words, a piece of flesh from the body of a participant is offered to the Creator during a Sundance. This is done during either the third or fourth day of a Sundance depending on which society is dancing. The Eagle society for instance dances for three days and three nights while the Buffalo society dances for four days and four nights. The dance and fasting that are included are also forms of sacrifice.

Traditionally among Aboriginal nations, the more valued a gift is, the greater the value it has in the spirit world. Even today, it is not uncommon for an elder to offer a rare sacred eagle feather to someone who is considered worthy. Not only is the recipient acknowledged, but so is the elder for giving up such a prized possession which they themselves had earned. In the Dakota tradition, someone who has sacrificed in the Sundance on behalf of the Creator over many years is given a Red Blanket to wear.

Sacrifice, as you can tell from the word, is related to the sacred aspects of life. And by definition, it is the act of making an offering (animal, plant, food, drink, or some other precious object) to a spiritual being. Therefore, it is the surrender of a precious article for the sake of something else that has greater value. Often it includes sacrificing something for an ideal, belief, or a specific purpose. In some cases, the sacrifice is placed on an alter, or other consecrated area; however, within Aboriginal cultures, since there is no separation between the sacred and the profane and all things are sacred, the alter may take various forms and the type of sacrifice can encompass a wide diversity of articles. In many cases, the act of suffering accompanies the sacrifice. This suffering is often contingent on the ceremony and the purpose of the sacrifice: the greater the suffering and sacrifice, the greater the benefit for the person, the community or the nation.

In the Dakota Eagle Society Sundance, we dance within a sacred alter, which is shaped like a nest. Like eaglets, we dance facing the Sundance tree, blowing our eagle whistles, crying for our spiritual sustenance. Through the sacrifice of fasting and offering our flesh on the third or fourth day, our prayers are answered.

Campbell (1988 :112) in his book *The Power of Myth,* wrote of the necessity of sacrifice to attain bliss (complete happiness and a connectedness to the Divine). Through sacrifice one can live in constant consciousness of the spiritual principle and experience the creative forces of life. Moreover, sacrifice can "remove man's mind from blind commitment to the goods of the world". Included in sacrifice is the contribution of women, something that Campbell omits. During the Sundance, they give themselves in sacrifice in support of the male dancers and the community. Amiotte (1990) also refers to this idea when he speaks of the transcendent quality of sacrifice.

Thus, sacrifice, be it small acts in the everyday existence of a person or the ceremonial acts performed once a year, can bring great benefits to a people: strengthening the ties that bind us, our nations and the earth; increasing our personal stamina to withstand the daily tribulations of life; and connecting us with the forces in the universe. Thus, sacrifices encompass a broad range of acts. A person gathering plants for medicines to heal the sick, the hunter searching for game to feed his family, a child looking for a special ability from a spirit helper, or an adult thanking the Creator for a special blessing in the Sundance, all are opening themselves up to a greater state of being. Sacrifice thus becomes a reminder that there are powers and forces in the universe that are greater than the person, and this humility unveils the other important values in life such as compassion for others. This is why during the transition ceremonies to adulthood there are sacrifices involved, it is through suffering and sacrifice that the soul can be awakened to compassion.

Sundancers begin the process of Sundancing, for various reasons, each person deciding for themselves what that is. For myself, it began after hearing A.C. Ross, a Lakota educator, explain how he had been given a gift during a *Yuwipi* ceremony (Blanket Ceremony) and was told that he would have to give something back in return. He promised that he would sacrifice a part of himself by Sundancing. I was in a similar situation having attended a *Yuwipi* Ceremony, and felt this was the best way for me to return something. I didn't begin by seeking out a Sundance. In a way it came to me. Dakota elder, Calvin Pompana, was holding a Sundance at Birds Hill Park north of Winnipeg the following year. I was informed that I would be welcome to participate in the Sundance. I made a choice to return something for the gift I had been given in the *Yuwipi* ceremony. At first I thought perhaps dancing a year would suffice, but I was informed that it was at the least a four -year commitment and perhaps for some, a lifetime. I decided that I would dance for four years and take each year at a time. The Sundance would require a sacrifice of food, water, flesh and most importantly time to the community and the Creator. It meant preparing for the Sundance a year before it occurred and then finalizing the commitment with a pledge that could not be broken. The culmination of the three days of fasting, praying, and dancing prepares one for the final act of sacrifice, the breaking away from the Sacred Tree and the sacrifice of ones own flesh on behalf of others. Another aspect of sacrificing is the death of ones ego, the concern for oneself during the act of sacrifice involves a certain way of looking at the world. Among many Aboriginal societies, sacred ceremonies were institutionalized by way of a vision quest.

The Vision Quest – A Personal Act of Sacrifice

At one time, the process began around the age of nine, when a child went into the woods for a short period of time to prepare for their vision quest later in life. During this time, they would learn what it was like to be deprived of the amenities of life, such as food and water. They would also learn to trust the spirits for protection. By the time male children reached the age of puberty, they were prepared to endure four days and three nights of fasting without food or water. Unlike the males, female children were required to go into isolation at the beginning of their first menstrual cycle and remain there until it ended. There they would learn the duties they would have to perform during womanhood. They were not required to sweat like the boys because of their natural means of purification that took place during the menstrual cycle. For myself, I would not go on a vision quest until I was thirty years old. That is because I was still a child in the ways of *Seeing the World with Aboriginal Eyes*.

During the vision quest a male child would enter the sweat lodge for the first time and be told the story of how a young boy had brought the sweat lodge to the people in order to heal them (Benton-Banai 1988). Every component of the vision quest is considered to be sacred and requires the sacrifice of something. When choosing the poles for the Sweat Lodge, or the gathering of stones, which are referred to as the Grandfathers due to their antiquity, the offering of tobacco is required before their use. In some Aboriginal traditions it is believed that if one doesn't show the proper respect to the Grandfathers when making an offering, the result would be the stones breaking up when they are placed in the sacred fire, which could hinder the ceremony.

The Sweat Lodge itself is created from willow poles bent into the shape of a dome. Years ago they were covered with furs and moss to prevent light from entering. Today, canvas is used. A shallow pit is dug several feet in front of the entrance where the fire is built. The Grandfather stones are than placed there to be heated. Another pit is dug inside the lodge where the white-hot Grandfathers will later be placed to purify the participants. When the elder pours water on the stones, purification occurs from the steam that results. Next, a trail of cedar, a medicine plant that provides healing and strength, is placed on the ground from the Sweat Lodge to the fire. Once this occurs those participating in the sweat are not to cross over its line. They must always go around it if they want to get to the other side.

Once all these preparations are completed, the elder prepares the boy, who will be fasting by telling him the story of how the Sweat Lodge came into existence. The elder places a drum known as the Little Boy a few feet from the entrance inside the lodge. One by one they enter the Sweat Lodge, first by greeting the Waterdrum with the customary, "*Boozhoo*"! Once inside the Sweat Lodge, the elder informs the young faster how to conduct himself during the four days and nights he will have to endure during the vision quest. Prayers are then said and songs sung. Once the sweat has been completed, the boy proceeds to his fasting lodge, which has been built at a place where he feels most comfortable. This will help him commune with the spirits. The place could be situated on a cliff or by a river or mountain. He sprinkles cedar boughs around his fasting lodge to ensure that malevolent spirits are prevented from entering the area of his lodge while he is in prayer.

During the first day of the fast, the boy is curious, wondering if anything is going to happen. He sits in contemplation praying that he will receive direction to his life. That first night it is difficult for him to sleep because of the anticipation of something occurring. It is rare that anything does occur this first night, as it is still early in the fast. Finally he goes to sleep, making sure that he faces the east during the night. The elder has informed him that if he faces the west, towards that land of the spirits, he may not return. He is awakened by the brightness of the early morning sun and feels the cool dew of the morning air. The boy now feels hunger setting in. It has been a full day and night since he has had food or water. He begins to observe his surroundings in a new light as the things that surround him become more vivid. He begins the process of developing a relationship with them. He is becoming one with them. Later that afternoon, the elder appears, asking him about his dreams and experiences the night before. Usually he tells him little, except that he is hungry. It is still early in the fast.

The second night arrives and the boy has his first moments of doubt and fear. In some cultures, this is referred to as the long night of the soul. Hunger has now set in and the boy wonders for the first time if he has the strength to make it. For the first time, he begins to face his own weaknesses and to see himself in a new light. He feels his body getting weaker as it slowly approaches death. This is the night that he may have a significant dream. Perhaps a loved one who has passed away will appear in the dream to offer him assistance. Another night passes, and by the next morning he has overcome some of his doubts. Although he is becoming weaker, the hunger doesn't seem too difficult to bear. His prayers become even more intense as the day goes on. Once again, the elder arrives to guide him in understanding his dreams. The boy is now in complete harmony with his surroundings. He feels a form of communication beginning to develop with the other forms of life that surround him. Two birds fly by, perhaps mates to each other. The boy wonders to himself, "Is this a sign that love is on the horizon?"

The third night arrives and the fast is drawing to a close. The boy feels a bit of disappointment that nothing significant has occurred. He begins to rest and his eyes come to a close, he is suddenly jolted awake by the sound of a loud growl ringing in his ears. He thinks to himself, "Has a bear or wolf entered my lodge?" He is paralyzed with fear and cannot move as he sees the form of something that is huge and has fur. Is he dreaming or is he awake he asks himself. It looks like a bear but there is something odd about it. Its head appears more straight up and its face flat. "Do I have anything to defend myself with?" Suddenly he wakes up and looks around and sees nothing and hears nothing. As vivid as it seemed, he asks himself, "Was it real or only a dream?"

One the fourth day, the elder arrives again. The boy tells him about what had occurred the night before. The elder remains silent and then tells the boy his fast is almost over. Later that day, the elder returns and says to the boy it is time to go back into the Sweat Lodge so that he may re-enter the world. Before leaving for the sweat, he asks the boy if there is anything that he witnessed during the night. The boy tells him about his experience. The elder gives the boy his first cup of cedar water. He hasn't had anything to drink for four days.

Taking part in the sweat are the elder's helpers. They enter the sweat lodge and after four days without food or water the boy is very weak. The sweat seems like it will never end. Finally, the elder tells the people in the Sweat Lodge, "Last night this boy was visited by the spirit of one of the ancient ones, the flat nose bear, and, if he accepts, from this time on he will always have a relationship with the bear." The elder turns to the boy and says to him, "Do you accept this clanship with the bear?" The boy answers in a weak voice, "I accept." The elder then tells the others, "The boy has given himself for four days to the spirits. We will no longer consider him a boy as he is now a man."

After the sweat is over, the young man is given some cedar to put in his moccasins and is told that others will be waiting for him with a feast. During the feast, the young man makes his last sacrifice by giving away items that he considers important. He gives them to the elder and all who helped him through the experience. The elder then tells everyone that he will now be known by a new name affiliated with his spirit helper, one that is for adults, and not for children.

This example illustrates how a new way of looking at the world is brought about in the young man, the purpose of sacrifice, and sacrifice as a necessary part to existence. Death of the self, the opening of the mind and heart to things greater than oneself, the connecting of oneself with the elements of the universe, and the gaining of compassion and incomprehensible nature of existence, are now open to the young man and to others through the act of sacrifice. My own vision was not as pronounced as the one above, probably because I started at a later stage in life. Nonetheless, the story above is based on an actual experience that I had in *Coming to Knowing* by way of sacrifice.

ABORIGINAL CONSCIOUSNESS

This section discusses Aboriginal consciousness. Jungian theories on the conscious, unconscious and the collective unconscious are used as tools to help define Aboriginal consciousness.

Understanding Aboriginal Consciousness

Human consciousness is still a mystery, even though there have been many theories put forth concerning the workings of the mind. Aboriginal consciousness may be even more of a mystery, but the linking of two concepts provides a better understanding of the idea of *Seeing the World with Aboriginal Eyes.* "Consciousness" is discussed from a western perspective and then from an Aboriginal perspective.

Consciousness, in psychology, is a term denoting awareness of ideas and feelings. Specifically, it is the capacity to know, perceive, or arrange ideas and feelings into a meaningful entity. The term is usually restricted to that part of mental life which involves the relation and reaction of the individual to the external world of which he is aware at any given time....In [Freud's]his system consciousness is that portion of the psyche which has come in contact with the external world, has reacted to it, and has been modified by it. Consciousness is thus the result of the interplay of continuously striving forces of our environment, (*Funk & Wagnalls Encyclopedia* 1998)

There are different levels of consciousness, this section refers to the level at which consciousness can be defined as the awareness of oneself and one's surroundings, the awareness of some influence, and the emotional awareness of an individual or a group. Freud and Jung say that "the existence of an "unconscious" [was] the reservoir of energy which the organism utilizes in its psychic life" (*Funk & Wagnalls Encyclopedia*). Other views say it is below the threshold of consciousness and it is a transition state through which information passes to the conscious level. No definitive western explanation encapsulates what exactly the unconscious is. Later, Freud's concepts on the conscious and the unconscious mind were modified by Carl Jung. A.C. Ross (1989), a Lakota educator and psychologist, relates his understanding of Jungian psychology:

> Dr. Jung declared that the mind can be divided into three levels... The top part of the psyche, or the mind, Dr. Jung called the conscious, also known as the ego. This is the active thinking part of the mind, the part you use when you're awake. Below that level he called the personal unconscious where all the memories since birth are. ...This area of the mind is repressed or suppressed. The lower level of the mind Dr. Jung called the collective unconscious. He felt that latent memory traces from your entire ancestral past are stored in this area (Ross 1989:11).

Jung purported that the conscious and the unconscious cooperate by communicating in a number of different ways, such as through dreams, trances and meditation (Ross 1989). These activities also play an important part of Aboriginal peoples' lives. Jung theorizes that dreams come:

> ...from the unconscious, penetrating [into the] consciousness. And since the unconscious portion of the mind cannot talk, when it penetrates consciousness, it comes in the form of symbols, thoughts and ideas (Ross 1989:12).

These symbols and thought patterns form the basis for the connection between the three levels of the mind. Ross (1989) speculates that the dreams and visions, that give a person focus and direction in life and that help the person in times of suffering, come through the aid of spirit helpers. If this is true, then perhaps Freud's and Jung's theories concerning the collective unconscious could be used in part to explain this, for:

> Sigmond Freud, the father of modern psychology, believed that one was born with a pre-determined base of information...Carl Jung also believed that a person was born with a pre-set base of knowledge, which he termed the collective unconscious (Ross 1989:26).

This knowledge base that is pre-set in the collective unconscious that "contains latent memory traces from your entire ancestral past" (Ross 1989:11) is a source of knowledge and enlightenment for an individual. Thus, the entirety of human consciousness is influenced by these unconscious levels of the mind. But human consciousness depends to a great extent on the culture and its associated concepts (Dennet 1992). Physicist David Peat (1996), believes that Aboriginal learning patterns are set when the children are very young. Like maps, the children absorb information by several means in their lives and then develop patterns in their heads based on that information:

> The Native map is learned in childhood. It is absorbed while sitting at the feet of elders and hearing their stories and songs. The map grows out of dance and ritual, out of the movements of the seasons, and the ceremonies of the group. This map in the head is not simply a plan involving contours, vegetation, and trails, for it expresses the group's place and their sense of harmony within the landscape...(Peat 1996:12)

Henderson (1992) uses the Mi'kmaq term, *Nstou'qnm* when referring to Algonquian consciousness; it means the indigenous life-long learning process. As children grow up, everything that is part of their environment is experienced and interpreted. Considering the fact that everything alive is considered holy and sacred, it is impossible to separate spirit from the everyday realities that exist in the Mi'kmaq view of the world. For instance, a ceremonial pipe in the Mi'kmaq language would be considered animate 'living'. Mi'kmaq conscious comprehends objects by the spiritual power that is contained within them as to whether they are alive or dead. Thus the Aboriginal conscious emphasizes different thinking processes than the western conscious.

Aboriginal educators, such as Ross (1989), believe that Aboriginal cultures may influence the utilization of certain parts of the brain over other parts that are stressed in western culture. He divides the brain into two hemispheres, the left being considered for ideas that encompass linear thought such as logic and mathematics. The right side of the brain emphasizes the intuitive. Traditional Aboriginal people rely on intuition for hunting and survival skills, while survival in the western world relies more on rational and reductive thinking; Aboriginal children are thus conditioned from an early age to develop the right side of the brain. This is not to say that Aboriginal people do not think logically or that Euro-Americans cannot be intuitive. Rather, due to cultural conditioning one is stressed more than the other.

From a traditional Mohawk perspective, one could use the analogy of the twins from the creation story when referring to left and right brain theories. The twins themselves are referred to as the left- and right-handed twins in Mohawk. The left-handed twin is always concerned with controlling the earth while the right-handed twin is always striving to be in the spirit world. Therefore, our minds are developed in much the same way depending on how one is influenced by culture. Culture shapes the learning patterns of the students, if we are taught to be left brain learners, our thinking patterns will be formed along that of the left-handed twin, one of dominance over cohabitation.

A number of educators have postulated that the western emphasis on technological advancement is beginning to shape the thinking patterns of Aboriginal peoples, altering their consciousness in a negative way. Some Aboriginal youth are struggling during the transition stage from a right brain over a more left-brain education system. Kremer, a psychologist, explains the difficulty Aboriginal people face in trying to retain their own forms of consciousness under the influences of the dominance of western consciousness.

> Consciousness is about something....we learn during the socialization process each culture provides. Socialization is training in understanding the world in a particular way.... The Western technological view, which has practically taken over how the world is understood almost everywhere, is thus created as a particular way of being in the world – and not, as too often assumed,

the only true way of being in the world,
freed from illusions and dogma (Kremer
1994:14).

Further, when Aboriginal people begin to lose their own
forms of understanding they may develop what is referred to as a false
consciousness. Marie Battiste refers to this as cognitive imperialism.
She defines it as the last stage of imperialism which results in one's
conscious being informed by the dominating, conquering 'other', such
as the colonizers (Barman *et al.*1986). There are a number of correlations
that one can make between Aboriginal understandings of consciousness
and Jungian psychology. One of the most controversial ideas that Jung
proposed is that the collective unconscious was a part of the psyche, just
as the personal unconscious was, but that it did "not owe its existence
to personal experience and consequently is not a personal acquisition"
(Campbell 1971:59). Essentially personal unconscious was made up of
elements that were once conscious but were now either suppressed or
disappeared from consciousness. On the other hand, elements of the
collective unconscious have never been conscious and not individually
acquired but rather acquired through ancestry and heredity. He
theorized that the collective unconscious was composed of archetypes
or primordial thought patterns that can become conscious and give form
to psychic contents, usually in a symbolic form (Campbell 1971:60).

....Universal thought forms known as archetypes are found
within the unconscious mind. .. Dr. Jung said the most common
archetypes existing within the collective unconscious of each
individual are: birth, rebirth, death, power, magic, unity, hero,
child, supreme being, shadow, wise man, earth mother, animal,
animus and anima (Ross1989: 27-28).

Since an archetype is considered to be an original pattern
of something, the Anishnawbe refer to them as their 'grandfathers',
Mishomis, others refer to their 'grandparents', and others refer to "walking
with the ancestors." Aboriginal people such as the Montagnais-Naskapi,
who are linguistically related to the Mi'kmaq and other Algonquian-
speaking groups, refer to archetype as *Mista'peo* (Big Man) (Speck
1963). The relationship with *Mista'peo* and other ancestral spirits can
be developed by fasting and dreams. These express themselves in the
conscious mind in symbolic form and were a result of the collective
unconscious transmitting knowledge to the conscious mind through the
personal unconscious. During vision questing, specially trained elders

interpret the meaning of dreams. In the past, some Aboriginal societies such as the Rotinonshonni held interpretation festivals to understand their dreams and the ancestors who appeared in them; failing to have a dream interpreted could result in imbalance leading to sickness and death. In the Shaking Tent Ceremony access is made to the ancestral spirits. The Northern Anishnawbe and Cree refer to the ancestral spirit of humans as *Wiisakechaahk*. Other ancestral spirits who may enter the Shaking Tent are the sun, turtle, ice, bear, strongman and the hairy chests, along with many other archetypes.

The archetypes or ancestral spirits of Aboriginal people are retained in the Aboriginal mind through story, ceremony and song. Over the years of learning, they become manifested over and over in the Aboriginal way of life where they are in turn passed on, unlike western culture where these facets of culture have been lost. Whether it is because they become embedded in the unconscious or, as Jung believed, that they are the archetypes of that particular culture and inherited from the ancestors, or even the ancestors themselves, the fact remains that they play an active role in the psychic life of an Aboriginal person. Campbell (1971:21) states the following about the roles that the archetypes and collective unconscious plays in retaining the well-being of a person.

> ... there is a way of thinking in primordial images, in symbols which are older than historical man, which are inborn in him from the earliest times, and, eternally living, outlasting all generations, that still make up the groundwork of the human psyche. It is only possible to live the fullest life when we are in harmony with these symbols; wisdom is a return to them. It is a question neither of belief not of knowledge, but of the agreement of our thinking with the primordial images of the unconscious (p.21).

The conscious, personal unconscious and the collective unconscious parts of the psyche all play an integral part in forming the Aboriginal consciousness; and they offer the Aboriginal person a way to be in harmony and balance with the physical and metaphysical realms of existence.

Chapter Four

NORTHERN DOOR:
WAYS OF DOING

A society's religion or spirituality has much to say about the rules of conduct and moral behavior that form the basis of its ethical decisions. The manner in which a society orders and arranges itself offers insight into the moral principles that guide that society. As each society fosters certain behaviors that maintain stability and harmony among its members, a study into ethical positions taken by a society will shed light on their particular ways of resolving issues. This section investigates several Aboriginal nations and examines the ethical positions the people living within them take, by referring to the values and beliefs that constitute the foundation of their ethical principles. It discusses the integration of traditional values with contemporary values.

Ethical and Moral Issues of the Red Road

Ethical positions are essential to consider when describing how people resolve issues that may disrupt the harmony in a community. Ethical positions are based on a people's understanding of their place within the universe. These are considerations to investigate when examining the ethical decisions of a culture. In the case of Aboriginal peoples, it is necessary to consider their connections with the environment and other-than-human persons. Cree hunters, for instance, hung the bones of the animals they killed in a tree, in order to appease the spirits of those animals. If animals are not shown proper respect they become angry and the hunters may face starvation.

Ethics are integral parts in the schemata of all peoples. They are the principles that guide individual persons and their societies to which they belong. These principles consist of specific rules of conduct associated with certain aspects of their lives. Therefore, when we speak of ethics and morals, we are studying the principles that guide that particular group of people. How individuals conduct themselves within their societies is scrutinized by the rest of the community, who decide how much respect will be given back to the member. Appointed leaders have an even greater responsibility towards the community than others. Thomas (1997) often joked that he wished he wasn't a chief because the responsibility was so great that he no longer could do what he wanted.

When considering the morals of people, identifying which values are deemed the most important is required. For instance, the Anishnawbe list seven such values. Dumont (1997) lists the Anishnawbe Seven Gifts of the Grandfathers as follows: respect, bravery, honesty, humility, truth, wisdom and love. Inherent in these values are also such concepts as: generosity, the ethic of sharing, the ethic of non-interference, kindness, and the maintenance of dignity, harmony and balance. In order to become initiated in the *Midewiwin* society, one has to practice these values for a full year. All societies whether Aboriginal or non-Aboriginal adhere to most of the values presented. When discussing values, it is the particular explanation placed on them by each culture that is important to consider; the cosmological rationale for the values as well as how their belief structures affect the expression of those values. For instance, there is nothing that Aboriginal peoples value more than their independence. The Rotinonshonni learned many years ago what the loss of freedom could mean to them when their nations were fighting among themselves. Thomas (1997) said that during this time people were afraid to leave their villages or walk at night. The Rotinonshonni value system was restored through the work of the *Peacemaker* and his companion *Ayenwatha*. They offered the people an alternative to violence based on a constitution called the *Kayeneren: Kowa*, (Great Law of Peace). This law restored freedom and liberty to the Rotinonshonni. Even today when greeting other members of the society, Rotinonshonni will say *Ske:nen kowa ken* meaning, are you still following the way of peace? This is a reminder to each other that each individual has a duty to ensure they continue to co-exist in peace.

The truths declared by the *Keyeneren: kowa* embodied more than a list of rules to live by; it embodied the very essence of our beliefs. Other Aboriginal nations also worked within confederacies and the duties and obligations expressed within their agreements were based on their cosmological orientation. Within these various confederacies there can be seen a particular orientation to the cosmos. For the Rotinonshonni, as well as other nations, this orientation encouraged individual freedom of the person and the nation. This can be seen in the way the people conducted their relations with others, for even in the confederacies different nations were not bound by any one body of authority. Each nation was autonomous and had the right to leave the confederacy if it couldn't agree with the other members. The purpose of coming together was to have a consensus based on mutual respect and understanding, even if everyone did not agree with the resolution. Therefore, if at the end of the day, everyone left the council with a mutual feeling of deference, the meeting would be considered for the most part a success.

This value of communal liberty also extended to individuals, as they were also free to make decisions for themselves, unless they were deemed detrimental to the community as a whole. For example, during times of war, individuals were asked if they wanted to join a war party. They were not coerced into joining and their decision was respected by the community. Individuals were cherished for their abilities and not for their weaknesses; for example, *Sagoya: watha* (Red Jacket) who ran away from battle was considered to be one of the great orators of the Seneca nation. Had the Rotinonshonni not recognized his gifts, they would have lost one of their great speakers. *Sagoya: watha,* would not have been able to fulfill his duty in life and been able to contribute to his society.

Liberty is a value that the early colonists in North America also wished to foster; it did not fit into the value systems of European nations and personal independence and liberty became a rallying point in the American Revolution. There has been much written about how the Rotinonshonni orientation on liberty influenced the American form of democracy. Lyons (1997) is only one such traditionalist and scholar to comment on this matter.

The duties towards family are also dictated by moral principles. For instance, five major functions of the family are: 1) economic (provision of goods and services for family members); 2) socialization of family members, particularly the young; 3) control of sexuality within the community and family; 4) emotional support and care; and 5) procreation. It is through these basic functions that we come to know the duties and obligations that are expected of us as members of a society. As they are expressed in culturally specific ways they are formally established in the cosmology of the culture. To illustrate this, we can refer to the cosmological orientation that many Aboriginal peoples have concerning their connection with the environment; that is; most of us have an affiliation with a certain animal or totem. This affiliation forms the basis of many moral decisions. Clan, lineage and kinship relations of community members is determined by oral traditions set down years before and the rules and regulations set by this ancient affiliation determines who can and cannot marry, who will be faith-keepers of a particular tradition, and who can hold particular positions in a society. Thus, the values held intact by the clan, extended family and lineage are supported through our spiritual beliefs. The ceremonies and doctrines are the foundation for the maintenance of order and stability within the nation. To ensure stability it is up to the individual to make sure that they conform to the laws.

Among some societies, such as the Rotinonshonni, clan affiliations have survived in spite of societal changes. The Anishnawbe have also retained some aspects of their clan affiliation, this is dependent on whether they are traditional or Christian in their beliefs. The Tewa, in some areas, still retain the cultural tenets that help identify them as traditional Tewa, with the clan still being the most important family identifier among them (Dozier 1966). On the other hand, Tewa living in urban centres do not have as strong a clan affiliation and often reside in nuclear families rather than the traditional extended clan family. This is true with other Aboriginal societies living both on and off reserve.

Today, many Aboriginal peoples are struggling to retain these components that bring cohesion to their communities. It has become an even greater problem in places where societies have been acculturated and no longer follow the guidelines set through traditions and beliefs. This struggle to retain traditional family values is reflected in an article by Niatum (1995). She reflects on her Tlingit family and the loss of culture resulting from her mother who became acculturated into Euro-American society. This conflict can also be seen in other changes that are occurring within contemporary Aboriginal nations.

Traditional roles about sexuality are also affected. Most Aboriginal societies have reserved a special place for cross-gendered persons. This is based on cosmological orientation, an example being male persons who are inclined towards female occupations and dress, are perceived to be destined towards their roles even before birth. In Anishnawbe, the common term is 'Agokway', in Cree 'Ayenkway' and in Dakota 'Winkté'. Unlike Aboriginal society today, there was no stigma attached to someone choosing to live contrary to the norms of the society, and in fact some were given special status within their society. The same goes for females who chose male roles over that of their own gender. There were several noted female warriors among Aboriginal groups. Often these men/women women/ men were considered to be third gender and special in their own right.

Today, a number of Aboriginal people are attempting to regain and revitalize the traditions of their ancestors. For many Aboriginal people the path back to their ancestral traditions is a slow one. The development of a relationship with the natural world is difficult for those brought up in the city. It requires that they search through their family genealogies and history's for moments of the past. Some return to their reserves later in life; others look to elders living in the city for traditional teachings (Stiegelbauer 1996). Elders are excellent teachers for those who have lost the spiritual path of their ancestors as they have experienced many of the stages of life and can provide direction and focus to the new generation. They feel a sense of duty to pass on their knowledge before it disappears forever.

Many nations have teachings stating that there will be a time when the traditions of their people will be restored. Anishnawbe believe that there will be a time when the people who have lost the traditional knowledge will begin to perform their ceremonies again, the time of the Seventh Fire. Then, the people will be renewed by the primal teachings of the Creator. The *Midewiwin* society of the Anishnawbe is helping those who choose to rekindle this lost knowledge or "Red Road". Part of the recovery process involves relearning the sacred stories so people find their spiritual centre (Brown 1996). If this trend continues, a resurgence of ethical and moral stances based on traditional knowledge and wisdom will occur.

All societies have rules and sanctions for those who disobey the rules, however, Aboriginal peoples had no prison systems and enforced their rules and laws in other ways. The maintenance of harmony between family and community members was of paramount importance. Since adultery upsets the balance of the community it was dealt with at a community level. Elders' resolved conflict by bringing the two parties and their clan families together. This restorative process is now being used by many non-Aboriginal organizations. Major crimes were also handled differently as restoration of harmony and balance among the community members was critical. Thus, the person who committed a crime needed to take responsibility for it, restore harmony through restitution if necessary and ensure the community that it would not be disturbed again. Justification for these actions is expressed in their teachings and traditions. Sometimes crimes were resolved through the intercession of elders or the clans to which the parties involved belonged. Or restitution might be paid to the victim of a crime in order to avoid an internal clan war. The absence of such a mechanism resulted in revenge killings. Thus, the coming of the *Peacemaker* to the Rotinonshonni Confederacy brought a means to resolve disputes in a peaceful manner.

The cosmology of each Aboriginal nation also affected the socialization of their children. The values based on traditions and customs become fixed in their personality so that when they became adults they behave in ways that befit the morals and ethics of their culture. Chance (1966) explains that the personality of an Inupiaq child is affected by culture. Hoebel (1978) states Cheyenne children learn how to behave through the example of their parents and community. For instance, they are taught that to be quiet and respectful in front of their parents is proper behavior. Not to do so would mean that the whole community would be aware of the situation and the child would be ostracized. In each case, there would be supporting teachings, stories and traditions that reinforce these behavior patterns.

Traditional teaching also ensured that each person would work on behalf of his/her people. Knowledge that was acquired was for the betterment of the whole community rather than for just oneself. In the past, respect was earned on how a person related and helped other members of his/her family and community. The choosing of traditional leaders on their ability and desire to help others is just one example of this. Traditional leaders had to be willing to give away most of their possessions in order to show the community that they were not superior to anyone else. Sometimes a chosen leader refused the position because of the responsibilities that went with the job. As a result, not everyone was willing or able to fulfill the role of a leader. Even today, you have to show that you can take care of your family before anyone will even consider you as a leader (Thomas 1997). This comes from the traditional belief that if you can't look after your own family, you will never be able to look after your people.

Hallowell (1967) tells us that the Anishnawbe individual was dependent on other-than-human beings in everyday activities. This belief also has a direct impact on the ethical and moral principles of the Anishnawbe, for they believe they can achieve a good life through the intercession of spirit beings related to nature. They feel it is their moral duty to try to exist in a state of *Pimadaziwin,* which means living life to the fullest. This is why *Nanabush* or *Misaboose* is represented as a Great Hare with the double entendre Great Light a being that intercedes when needed. Anishnawbe and other Algonquian groups believe human beings to be the most dependent species on earth and, as a result, must rely on others to fulfill their needs. That dependence is oriented towards setting a path that leads to a life as good as possible in this reality rather than in the afterlife.

Anishnawbe believe that everything in existence has already been developed in the spirit world and that inspiration is a result of contact with knowledgeable spirits on dreams. Traditional Anishnawbe believe that inventions are not a product of human ingenuity but already exist within the realms of the spirit world. Speck (1963) asked a Montagnais person why Montagnais were not advanced like the European technology if every invention pre-exists. The response was Montagnais didn't need more as they had everything they needed. Thus, we see the concept of humility and the idea that greed was immoral being advanced for it was inappropriate and wrong to advance ideas that led to self-glorification.

The spirits who give the Anishnawbe direction and focus in life are referred to as grandfathers; there were obligations on the part of Anishnawbe towards these grandfathers. This belief is so strong that many feel that if they do not meet these obligations, it could result in illnesses to themselves or their families. Many Aboriginal peoples believed that being ill was a punishment due to transgressions against spirit helpers. One outcome of this belief was that many missionaries kept reminding them that they were being punished for their improper social conduct; that is, the traditional ethics and morals that guided them were immoral and unethical. As a result, many converted to Christianity when previously unknown plagues swept through their villages.

Hallowell (1967) points out that one way to be restored to health was through confession, and this aspect of Christianity proved to be attractive to suffering Anishnawbe. However, to confess in order to restore health also meant to convert to Christianity. This did little to alleviate the suffering of afflicted Aboriginal people, who were then taught that this was an advancement into heaven by the priests who were themselves not afflicted by the same diseases. Even in cases such as this, Aboriginal converts to Christianity believed fully that they had a duty to share these teachings with others. Today the most stringent Christian ministers in the north are often Aboriginal people.

The values that Aboriginal peoples held were reflected in their stories. Thomas (1997) states all Rotinonshonni values are rooted in the creation story. Asikinack (1987) explains stories told by the Anishnawbe embody their earliest traditional values. He notes the correlation between the *Windigo* complex and the human vice of gluttony. To hoard was considered a form of sorcery, one could be accused of being *Windigo* like, as only a *Windigo* would deprive others of food. Even today, in some Algonquin communities along the Ottawa River, the freezer is referred to as the "stingy box" because it is seen as a place where meat is hoarded rather then shared.

As spiritual constructs form the basis of moral conduct, it is important to note how particular individuals in a society ensure that the rules of conduct are adhered to. The rules of conduct and the manner in which Aboriginal societies arrange themselves is guided by moral principles that are embedded in spiritual constructs that in turn are expressed in the actions of individuals. This is crucial to understanding Aboriginal cultures as these spiritual beliefs promote behaviors within society that maintain stability, harmony and balance. Thus, a study into ethical positions taken by Aboriginal peoples can shed light on their societies' world view, cosmology and value system, as these constitute the foundation to their ethical and moral principles.

SEEKING THE SACRED REALM

This section illustrates the path of life taken by *Kesheyanakwan*, Art Solomon, an Anishnawbe elder. His own personal search for the meaning of life, his analysis of the world around him, and his thoughts on the past, present and future world and his people will be examined. Every culture and tradition has people born into it who are destined to live a life of service for the betterment of their people. Most of the modern religions can trace their development to the presence of individuals who have contributed significantly, and, as a result of these people's lives, their community, nation and the world have altered in ways that have improved humankind. In previous sections, we have mentioned the *Peacemaker*, Handsome Lake and Jacob Thomas among the Rotinonshonni. They were either social reformers or teachers whose ideas and teachings brought transformation or knowledge to my society.

Reaching Fulfillment

There are also those members of society whose life of service is directed to the betterment of individuals which in turn strengthen the nation. They seek no reward for their work, their influence is often more subtle than social transformers of a grand scale. Nonetheless, they are extremely important to the well-being of a people and their community. Often they have become social activists who dedicate their lives to their society by performing altruistic acts. Their work leaves such an impression on others that their influence remains long after they have passed on.

But what sustains these people? What forms the basis of their philosophy that enables them to carry on this work? What is present in their world view that necessitates this response to the trials and tribulations of the disadvantaged? How can we learn about the underlying motivations of these people so that we can understand the sources of their strength? These questions and others need to be investigated if we are to understand how this philosophy of life manifests itself.

A person's philosophy of life stems from conceptual frameworks that are based on culture, ethos and world view. A person derives meaning to their existence through these elements. For some, such as Solomon, they may present a vision of the world that is at odds with mainstream cultures, and therefore form a basis for an alternative direction in life, a direction that differs from that promoted by the majority of society. Furthermore, a person's knowledge of his/her own philosophy increases their knowledge of self, and may change their perception of reality on numerous levels of existence.

A person who has given much of their life for the betterment of others has a strong sense of self and a well-formed and thought-out philosophy of life, often found through years of contemplation and introspection. Solomon's philosophy was based on traditional knowledge and teachings of his people. As you proceed to learn about Solomon, and his work with the disadvantaged, consider what made him the person that he was, what aspects of his life influenced his actions and in what ways he derived meaning for his existence from self-knowledge and traditional knowledge. Most of all, try to determine how he reached fulfillment in his life and what leading a fulfilling life meant to him. But first let's look at some general information concerning his life.

Solomon spent his life working on behalf of the down-trodden, attempting to liven up their spirits so that they could once again be proud members of their society. Although brought up as a Roman Catholic, he was also involved with members of the *Midewiwin Society*, but was never formally initiated into it. This Society is one of the upholders of Anishnawbe tradition, and although it was suppressed up to the 1950's by the government of Canada and as late as the 1970's in the United States, it has made a revival in many Anishnawbe communities. The *Midewiwin* members are committed to serving their people by instilling pride, through songs, stories and ceremonies. They follow a strict moral code of conduct, with adherents to the Society pledging them selves to work on the restoration of the Anishnawbe culture on behalf of their people.

Solomon was able to straddle the fence between people of both Traditional and Christian beliefs. So respected did he become, that he was the only Aboriginal person to be selected by the World Council of Churches in 1983, to bring Aboriginal values to representatives of other faiths.

However, it is not his work with the people of other faiths that he will be remembered, but rather with those who had lost their faith in living. *Kesheyanakwan* dedicated his life to the restoration of lives lost to the prison system. He also worked in support of women recovering their rightful place as leaders in their societies. In his youth, he had witnessed the domestic violence that was occurring at alarming rates in Aboriginal communities, as a result of the legacy of residential schools. Solomon knew that violence was a contributor to the high incarceration rates of Aboriginal people. As a product of the residential school system, he tirelessly spoke out to the governments and churches who had disrupted the social equilibrium of the Aboriginal societies with there patriarchal imposed forms of family, leadership and government. He was often subject to criticism by both Aboriginal and non-Aboriginal males, who saw him as a threat. But Solomon was not one to back down like others who had gone before him, who were easily bought off with government jobs.

According to Solomon Aboriginal women in the United States and Northern Canada were deliberately sterilized during the 1960's and 1970s. One-third of the Aboriginal women in mid-western United States who gave birth were deliberately sterilized. In Canada this subject is suppressed by the government and the media. Solomon mentioned he could get the documents from a nurse who had worked in the Yukon and Northwest Territories who had witnessed the procedure; however, no members of the media ever wanted to get involved with the issue as it was politically too explosive.

Solomon became a leader in the American Indian Movement (AIM) in the 1970s. He took a strong stand against the wishes of a number of Aboriginal leaders, regarding weapons being used as a means of protest. But he never backed down in stating what he believed, and differences in opinion did not prevent him from doing what he felt was right. When American Indian Movement member Leonard Peltier was falsely convicted of killing two FBI agents at Wounded Knee in 1975, Solomon was there for moral support. Unfortunately, 28 years later, Peltier still remains in prison, in spite of the evidence of his innocence.

Solomon was responsible for bringing Aboriginal elders and ceremonies into Canadian prisons. As a result of his relentless efforts based on the constitutional right to practice one's faith traditions, many inmates for the first time were exposed to the truth and beauty of their culture. The pipe and the sweat lodge became part of the fabric of rehabilitation for Aboriginal inmates in some Canadian prisons. One inmate commented that it was too bad that he had to go to prison to learn about his culture. But due to the dedication of those such as Solomon, some inmates are able to leave prison more whole than when they first entered. Unfortunately, too often this was not the case, for spiritual leaders had many obstacles put in their path by the prison bureaucracies who seemed more interested in handing out punishment than rehabilitation. For instance, when elders arrived at the prisons to visit the inmates, healing pipes would be confiscated and checked for drugs. Meanwhile Christian clergy would enter the prison with no checks to their person or belongings. Solomon spoke out against this double standard even at the risk of undoing the positive steps that had already been taken in alleviating some of the inequities.

Solomon was an advocate for Aboriginal inmates. Often he

became frustrated by what he knew to be happening in prison life after the doors closed behind him. Nonetheless, with the dedication of others such as Ed Newbery, Nahum Kanhai, Mel Bass and many others, along with the support of the *Midewiwin* Society, they were able to get the first official Halfway House started in Canada in the city of Sudbury for Native inmates. Newbery House has helped released inmates to adapt to life after incarceration through its philosophy based on the spiritual traditions of the Anishnawbe. As a result of this opportunity, many men who have gone through the doors of Newbery House have left and entered society as productive members. At Newbery House, Solomon, was often looked upon as a wise elder by both inmates and staff alike. However, even in those institutions that he helped establish, his distaste for hypocrisy put him at odds with members who controlled those institutions. Another significant contribution of Solomon was his initiation of the Native Studies Program at the University of Sudbury. Many Aboriginal peoples have graduated from this program and are now helping their own people. Among those is Native Studies professor Emily Faries. She, like Solomon, has been a recipient of the Aboriginal Achievement Award.

Solomon is one who became designated as an elder by members of his community. "Elder" is a title based on respect rather than age. It is bestowed upon very few. An elder exemplifies a person on the fourth stage of the Wheel of Life. Elders earn the respect of the people by providing assistance to them that is beyond the regular measure of being simply helpful or available. Solomon finished his book with a quote that succinctly states how he approached his journey on the path of life:

> ...I understood, you know, for a number of years that my responsibility in this world is to do the best that I possibly can do and to leave the rest to the Creator. So I can say to hell with it. I've done what I could do today and that's all (Solomon 1994:140)

Through this limited biographical sketch of Arthur Solomon and his writings, we can learn about his personal search for the meaning of life, and his analysis of the world around him. This glimpse into his heart and soul offers a unique opportunity to understand that the Aboriginal experience can offer a basis for an alternative direction in contemporary society.

TRADITIONAL KNOWLEDGE
SPECIALISTS - SHAMANS

Shamanism dates back to time immemorial and is a valued and respected aspect of many traditions throughout the world. Shamans are people who are:

> Mystical, priestly and political figure [s]...healers, seers and visionaries...in communication with the world of the gods and spirits...poets and singers... repositories of the knowledge of the culture's history, both sacred and secular. They are familiar with cosmic as well as physical geography; the way of plants, animals and the elements...They are psychologists, entertainers and food finders. Above all, however, shamans are technicians of the sacred and masters of ecstasy (Halifax 1979:3-4).

This section explores shamanism within Aboriginal cultures. Unfortunately, the word shaman is now often equated with the New Age Movement which complicates the validity of the word. More appropriate terms might be medicine person or traditional healer. However, these terms relegate these persons to specific activities. A shaman may have a variety of abilities such as a herbal healer, elder, medium, or spiritual practitioner. In this section I will use the term 'traditional healers' or 'specialists' in place of the general term 'shamans' unless I revert to a general understanding, then I will use the term 'shamans'.

Those Who Balance the Opposites

In previous sections, we have mentioned spiritual realms, ceremonies, sacrifice and initiation. In this chapter we see how all of these are manifested in the human journey that involves the death and renewal of an individual's psyche. This includes a peeling away of one's former existence and a remaking of the person. After a person has gone through the process of initiation, they can become spiritual leaders. They have learned to travel within the spiritual realms of existence, and in them, they are given instructions on how to bring balance to others who may be suffering from sickness or distress. Through an intensive training they acquire abilities that others lack. They become the medium between beings who inhabit different worlds.

Traditional knowledge specialists go through a period of

initiation that may require great asceticism on their part. This period could involve fasting as long as thirty days with only a small amount of food and water. For others, the knowledge is inherited and passed on from one generation to the next. The abilities that they receive, often comes from a family member who is about to pass to the next world. In some cases, the spirits begin to prepare the initiate to go through a period of great suffering, such as an illness before they receive the gifts of healing. As they pass through this difficult stage and then become well, they have acquired the spiritual and mental fortitude to be keepers of this sacred knowledge.

For some, the knowledge that they receive is considered a blessing while others are more reluctant to receive the gifts, as they may feel a sense of unworthiness in having the responsibility of caring for the knowledge of the culture. They may even try to deny this calling, for in some traditions it may require that they take on feminine characteristics and dress. Eventually those who accept become accustomed to their calling, and they may even end up taking on lovers who are physically the same as them, but are not considered of the same gender. That is because, they are said to have been imparted with a separate gender or may even be bi-gendered through spiritual intervention. Some do this to be in balance with the masculine and feminine aspects of human nature giving them a unique perspective on the world. A traditional healer who is born a male may need to experience the feminine side of himself in order to be in complete balance with himself. The same may hold for a female healer who may take on the male characteristic of a warrior. Others may deny their calling and get on with their lives in a normal fashion. However, to do so and to not follow their calling could result in danger and misfortune. Most end up accepting what is considered their destiny in order that harm doesn't come to themselves or their family.

For Aboriginal societies living in the north, he/she was not just a healer, but also an important component in the livelihood of their community. His/Her abilities were utilized to help find needed game for the community's sustenance. Cree shamans called *Miteo* in Northern Quebec, refer to the ceremony that aids them in hunting, as *Kwashapjigan*, which means seeing beyond the world. It resembles seeing through a window. By performing this ceremony, the *Miteo* is able to invoke the spirits that can aid his/her people in the hunt. Today this is referred to as the Shaking Tent Ceremony. It is rarely used nowadays as the traditional hunting way of life has almost disappeared. Most Aboriginal people in the north, no longer require the aid of spirit entities to help them in their hunt for food as they have other means of sustenance. Others still, believe the practice is an important component of their culture and should be retained. Today some Aboriginal people in Toronto and Winnipeg have put a modern spin on the ceremony and are utilizing it to help link Aboriginal families with their children who had been adopted out into non-Aboriginal families by child and family services or to help cure illnesses.

Those that perform the Shaking Tent Ceremony are referred to as "*Jeeskeewin*" in Anishnawbe and as mentioned *Miteo* in Cree. The lodge in which they perform the ceremony is similar to the Sweat Lodge; however, it is much higher with an opening at the top where the spirits may enter. The poles that make up the lodge are gathered from a variety of trees such as: poplar, tamarack, birch, cedar, spruce, and pine. They must come from a tree that is in the prime of its life. The ground that the ceremony is performed on should be pure and undisturbed by others. The poles are covered with a canvas.

Once inside the lodge, the healer continually smokes tobacco in order to appease the spirits that enter. Those who witness the ceremony are gathered around the lodge. They offer tobacco under the canvas and ask the spirits for answers to questions that are troubling them. They are then given answers through the *Jeeskweewin* who acts as a mediator between the people and the spirits. The name, Shaking Lodge, comes from the shaking that occurs to the lodge when the spirits enter it. The lodge is lit up by the embers of the pipe that the *Jeeskeewin* smokes. Through the silhouette created by this light, one is able to see the shadows of the *Atisokanak* that enter: the moose, turtle, fox and most importantly *Mista'peo*, the Great Man for the Innu named *Wiisakechaahk* by the Cree.

The best traditional healers come from youths who have not had sexual relations. They are considered to be unblemished by the spirits and therefore much more susceptible to acquiring their powers. The spirits themselves are willing to do whatever bidding the shaman asks of them. However, if the shaman performs the ceremony to invoke the spirits to harm others, the spirits will warn him and there will be consequences that he will have to face in the future. Due to the introduction of Christianity and the actions of a few bad shamans the Canadian government prohibited Aboriginal spiritual practices.

There are those who still fear bear walkers. These are said to be shamans who utilize the dark side of shamanism and take the form of animals to harm others. Their spirits never recover from this and they lose any chance of coming back to humanity forever. Instead of healing they do harm. Western society in the past referred to them as witches. Unfortunately, due to Christianity any one involved in the healing arts were designated as witches including traditional healers.

A tool often employed by shamans is the drum. By singing songs which are given to him/her in dreams and trances, a shaman is able to see into the drum events that are about to occur. The drum and songs also inform the spirits they are needed by a traditional healer. By seeing into the drum, it is believed that the traditional healer knows events that are about to occur such as when a death will come to them or when a person will make a permanent transition into the next life. Unlike most of us, they have little fear of death. They spend their lives traveling between the different realms of existence and in communication with spirits of those realms. To them, death is simply a final stage in the transition from this world to the next.

At one time all Aboriginal societies had their traditional healers, today there are only a few that still practice. They are either revered or feared by others. They have acquired their good reputations by the work that they have done with others in their life and remain humble and out of the limelight. They help to restore the balance in the lives of those who are sick. Their reputation transcends any race or nationality that they belong to, as they have gained the respect of both Aboriginal and non- Aboriginal people for their ability to heal.

One traditional healer who became controversial during one of my Traditional Knowledge Program residencies was the Inupiaq healer, Ralph Amouq, Gray Wolf. He informed our traditional knowledge class while we were in residency in Atlanta, Georgia that after a twenty-five year period of training in the ways of a traditional healer in Alaska, he had a vision that he should go south and help other potential healers to channel their abilities. His vision told him that one-day he would end up in Atlanta, Georgia. With three hundred dollars in his pocket he headed for Europe. While there he had no place to turn and one day with little food or money left, he was sitting by the dock in Germany when someone tapped him on the shoulder. The man asked Gray Wolf if he was a Native American. Gray Wolf told him that he was an Inupiaq from Alaska and was trained as a traditional healer. Soon after Gray Wolf was invited to a conference to discuss traditional healing to a group of German academics. Out of this experience grew a clientele who sought his council for physical, mental and spiritual healing. As his reputation grew, this enabled Gray Wolf to travel around the world where he met other healers and even some world leaders. After four years on the road, Gray Wolf landed in Atlanta Georgia where he began training potential shamans in the ways of healing. Gray Wolf said that as long as you trust the spirits, all of your needs will be taken care of. However, I wanted to add that all of the Aboriginal women in our Traditional Knowledge Program were wary of him and did not participate in his sessions. The non-Aboriginal women on the other hand sought him out for advice. I asked one of the female Aboriginal students as to why she didn't trust him. She explained, "I have seen his kind before in my community." One reason I have included Gray Wolf in this section is that there seems to be no doubt that he had some healing ability. He also had his weaknesses and this might have negated some of his abilities as a healer and the Aboriginal females in the program were intuitively able to pick up on it. Traditional healers are not always perfect people and we should be careful when we put them on a pedestal before knowing more about them. There are others who are able to overcome their own shortcomings and become powerful healers. They sacrifice much of their personal lives on behave of others. It is important that anyone interested in acquiring the services of a person in the traditional healing arts must always be wary of whom they seek for advice or learning.

Thus, this ancient tradition is still of relevance today. In fact, over the years traditional knowledge specialists and healers (shamans) bring harmony and balance within Aboriginal societies.

THE INWARD JOURNEY

The importance of the inner life to Aboriginal peoples is well documented. This inner reality and the quest to connect with the truths from this inner space alters consciousness and transforms the person into a "human." In essence, this inner life can teach each person much about his/her own strengths and weaknesses and offer direction and focus in life. But Aboriginal epistemology is more than simple knowledge. It is translated into the everyday behaviour of the people -- into their world view and culture. This section offers us one final insight into the operation of the Aboriginal mindset and one final glimpse into the *Aboriginal Way of Seeing the World.*

Find Our Place on the Journey of Life

In this book, like the four hills of life, childhood, adolescence, adulthood and elderhood, you have read through four paths within the circle of life as presented by Dumont (1997). There is the seeing path in the east; the path of relationships in the south; the knowing path in the west and the doing path in the North. The last section of the doing path is one that best encompasses the inward journey. Ermine (1995) believes that it is the inward path that one takes that distinguishes most Aboriginal knowledge systems from western knowledge systems.

I have included information from Campbell (1988) and others

to illustrate that Aboriginal forms of reality are not exclusive to just Aboriginal people's of the America's. Rather, that there is a commonality in understanding that exists among Aboriginal peoples both past and present that exist throughout the world. Within these varied traditions are the symbols that result from the seeking of inner truths which define the individual traditions of the cultures. As Campbell (1988) notes the human being has not evolved physically in over thirty thousand years. What has changed is that western knowledge based on technology has advanced by leaps and bounds in the past few centuries. This form of knowledge has progressed throughout every part of the world. What is being lost in this process is knowledge that is learned through introspection such as the introspection practiced through prayers, dreams and meditation. Ermine (1995) believes knowledge based on Aboriginal epistemologies are as important to the world we live in today as is western knowledge. In fact, due to the depletion of natural resources it may become the most important knowledge in leading us back into recognition that we are dependent on them for sustainability.

Like many other Aboriginal philosophers, Ermine (1995) believes we are losing our connections with other beings inhabiting the world. Our over-emphasis on technology has resulted in humankind being disconnected from the other realities. Grobsmith (1981) believes that even though Aboriginal peoples such as the Lakota have had to change and adapt to an ever-evolving world, they have retained their connection to the other forms of life as well as their beliefs in creation and the Creator. The idea that exists among them, that we are all united in a common destiny, is still prevalent in Lakota thought. *Mitakuye Oyasin* means we are all related and is a fundamental principle of Lakota philosophy.

There are some who believe that unless we begin to learn certain lessons from Aboriginal epistemologies, we may cease to exist in the future. Rather then setting ourselves apart from the rest of creation as has been done in the western philosophies, we must start working in co-existence with the rest of creation once again. Western society may even have to rethink its understanding about their belief in God.

Unlike the Judaeo-Christian God the Aboriginal Creator is not separated from the physical creation. The Lakota include sixteen deities that exist in the physical world that are the core components of the Great Spirit. Together they make up a sacred hoop that encompasses all aspects of Lakota reality (Grobsmth1981).

Only by way of understanding and by coming into relationship with all sixteen deities do the Lakota believe that we can grasp the full dimension of the Creator. All of the sixteen components that make up the Creator include phenomena that exist in our physical world. Each of the sixteen is prayed and meditated on through ceremonies that can be done daily or at certain times of the year. Each of them are performed in order for the Lakota to retain their connection with the fullness of the Creator. The sixteen components while divided remain a mystery to the seeker of answers to creation; together they become a sacred unity and are referred to as the Great Spirit by the Lakota. Only through meditation and prayer can one be in relationship with all of them. The distinctions between the sixteen begin to cease the deeper one delves into the mystery that lies within oneself. As the distinction becomes less between creation, the more unified one becomes with the Creator.

Other Aboriginal societies have a similar understanding of their inner relationship to the rest of creation and the Creator as the Lakota do. In the physical world we see the distinctions that exist between the different things that exist in the world. However, we know that this is only an outward manifestation of something that lies deeper and is more whole. It is the traditional healers of the different societies who best connect with the inner and outer realities that exist in the spirit world. Even individual forms no longer remain distinct from each other. As he/her weaves their conscious mind between the earth and the spirit worlds, spirits of the trees appear to him/her in the form of humans, while humans take the form of animals. Plant spirits offer him/her songs for healing while drums become windows to other worlds. It is we as human beings who see the distinctions between things.

Each society interprets their realities according to the dictates of their cultures. However, there is a commonality that exists in the core archetypes of each of the Aboriginal cultures. The Great Tree of Peace, said to be a Great White Pine to the Rotinonshonni, may be referred to as the Tree of Life, by another culture such as the Anishnawbe who may view it as being a Cedar Tree due to the Cedar tree's importance in the area they inhabit. Through spiritual insight they see the unity of all trees in their own cultural archetype. The Sundance Pole of the Lakota becomes the symbol of the archetypal Tree of Life. The planting of the Great White Pine of the Rotinonshonni at *Onondaga* becomes their representative archetypal tree and can be found as well in their story of creation. The tree becomes a unifying component of the people in each of their cultures. The symbols are universal ones which are viewed from each society's individual perspective.

In order to understand the true significance of a tree, one has to be able to search within, what Jung refers to as collective memory that exists in the deep levels of each individual's unconscious. This requires a deeper form of introspection than thought. Training begins at an early age so that when a child has approached adulthood they have already developed the skills and patience that are required in order to look deeply into the abyss of his/her inner mind. After they have looked deep enough, they then begin to see a unity of layers of the mind where separation exists. The collective unconscious, where lie all the archetypes soon begins to replace the personal unconscious. The individual is left with the community's interpretation of what they view in the collective unconscious.

Unlike Jung's understanding, the collective unconscious of the Aboriginal person is a doorway to a universal consciousness that transcends both space and time. It is where one can find all the elements that are in the creation stories of Aboriginal peoples. The stories that have evolved from this are known as *Atisokan* in Anishnawbe or what are referred to as cosmological stories. It is where the great cosmological beings of creation can be found. The heroes that are part of this component of oral tradition such as *Nanabush*, *Wiisakechaahk* or *Teharonhia:wako* reside in this place. They are remembered in the past but exist within the present. Few today are able to enter this place to seek them out for the doorway has been closed for most. We no longer take the time to search deeply enough inside ourselves to find the opening. The dreaming societies that exist are being replaced by television and videos. Mythical stories with little spiritual relevance are created out of these forms of technology to replace the oral stories that were told and retold for generations in the past. Long hours are spent idling the time away in front of the television. Many of us no longer believe that by looking inside ourselves we can find answers to unresolved questions. There are only a few who even try to make the attempt today.

In recent years there has been a change that is taking place. From the 1960s until today, there are those looking inside themselves in order to connect with the universal conscious. They are not only Aboriginal peoples, but others as well who are seeking answers through ancient teachings. They are on a search to know themselves better and to have a better relationship with the world they live in. To do this they have had to change the way they previously saw their place in the world. With patience, prayer and meditation, they are only now beginning to understand in part what it is like to "*See the World with Aboriginal Eyes.*"

References Cited

Adamson, Rebecca. 1992. Investing in Indigenous Knowledge. *Akwekon J.* *9*(2):50-51.

Alcoze, Thom. 1980. Professor of Native Studies, University of Sudbury. Personal communication.

Amiotte, Arthur. 1990. Giveaway for the Goods: An interview with Arthur Amiotte. *Parabola 15*(4):38-39.

Amouq, Ralph. 1997. Inupiaq Elder, Traditional Knowledge Doctoral Program. California Institute of Integral Studies. Personal communication.

Anonymous. 1992. *Cree Trappers Speak.* James Bay, ON: Waskaganish School Curriculum.

Asikinack, William. 1992. Anishinabe Legends through Anishinabe Eyes. *In* Millar, D.R, Beal, C, Dempsey, J., and Heber, R. W. (Eds.), *First Ones: Readings in Indian/Native Studies.* Piapot Reserve #75: SIFC.

Barman, Jean, Hebert, Yvonne, and McCaskill, Don. 1989. *Indian Education in Canada.* Vancouver, BC, University of British Columbia Press.

Barreiro, Jose. 1992. The search for lessons. *Akwe:kon Journal, 11*(2): 20-39.

Battiste, Mary. 1992. Micmac Literacy and Cognitive Assimilation. *In* Barman, J., Hebert, Y., and McCaskill, D. (Eds.), *Indian Education in Canada, Vol. 11: The Challenge.* pp. 57-63. Vancouver: UBC Press.

Benten-Banai, Edward. 1979. *The Mishomis Book.* St. Paul, MN: Red School House.

Bird, Louis. 2000. Cree Elder. Personal communication.

Brown, Joseph Epes. 1996. *The Sacred Pipe: Black Elk's Account of the Seven Rites of the Oglala Sioux.* Norman OK: University of Oklahoma Press.

Brown, Joseph Epes. 1982. *The Spiritual Legacy of the North American Indian Religions: American Indian Living Religions.* New York, NY: Crossroad.

Brown, Joseph Epes. 1969. The sacred pipe. *In* Black Elk, *Wiwanyag Wachipi: The Sun Dance.* p. 31. Norman, OK: University of Oklahoma Press.

Brown, Jennifer and Brown, Robert. 1990. *The Orders of the Dreamed: George Nelson on Cree and Northern Ojibwae Religion and Myth.* Winnipeg, MB: University of Manitoba Press

Bruchac, Joseph. 1993. Digging into your heart. *Parabola 18*(4): 34-41.

Cadato, Micheal J. and Bruchac, Joseph. 1991. Teacher's guide to keeper of the animals. *Native American Stories and Environmental Activities for Children.* Saskatoon: Fifth House Publishers.

Campbell, Joseph. 1988. *The Power of Myth.* New York: Doubleday.

Carpenter, Edmond. 1978. Silent music and invisible art, *Natural History*, *87*(5): 90-96.

Chance, Norman A. 1966. *The Eskimo of North Alaska.* New York: Holt, Rinehart and Winston.

Cleaver, G. (Ed.) 1974. *Selected Poetry of Duncan Campbell Scott.* Ottawa: The Tecumseh Press.

Colorado, Pamela. 1988. Bridging Native Science and Western Science. *Convergence, 21*(2/3): 49-68.

Copet, Wayne. 1992. An approach to community planning in Aboriginal settlements. *Canadian Journal of Native Studies 12*(1):37-50.

Cornelius, C. 1992. Thanksgiving address: Expression of Haudenosaunee worldview. *Akwe-kon J. 9*(3):14 –25.

Deloria, Vive. 1994. *God is Red.* Golden, CO: Fulcrum Publishing.

Dennet, Daniel C. 1992. *Consciousness Explained.* London UK: Penguin.

Dozier, Edward P. 1966. *Hano, A Tewa Indian Community in Arizona,* NY: Holt, Rinehart & Winston.

Dumont, James. 1997. Anishinawbe Traditional Knowledge Teacher, and Professor of Native Studies, University of Sudbury. Personal communication.

Eliade, Mircia. 1961. *Images and Symbols.* New York: Sheed & Ward.

Ermine, Willie. 1995. Aboriginal epistemology. *In* Battiste, M. and Barman, J. (Eds.), *First Nations Education in Canada: The Circle Unfolds.* pp. 101-112. Vancouver, BC: UBC Press.

Foster, Michael K. 1974. From beyond the earth to beyond the sky: An ethnographic approach to four longhouse Iroquois speech events. Canadian Ethnology Service, Paper No. 20: 109-114. National Museum of Man, *Mercury Series.* Ottawa, ON: National Museums of Canada.

Funk and Wagnalls Encyclopedia. 1998. New York NY.

Giese, Paula. 1996. www.kstrom.net/isk/stars/startabs.html Lakota Star Knowledge

Golindo, Mazalt. 1996. Traditional Knowledge Residency. Ph.D. Program. Mexico City: Mex. Personal communication.

Goodman, Ronald. 1992. *Lakota Star Knowledge: Lakota Stellar Theology.* Rosebud, SD: Sinte Gleska Univ.

Grobsmith, Elizabeth S. 1981. *Lakota of the Rosebud.* New York, NY: Holt, Rinehart, and Winston.

Hallowell, Irving A. 1967. *Ojibwe World View: Culture and Experience.* New York: Schoken Books.

Halifax, Joan. 1979. *Shamanic Voices: A Survey of Visionary Narratives.* New York, NY: Viking Penguin.

Henderson, Sa'kej James. 1992. *Algonquin Spirituality: Balancing the Opposites.* Mi'kmaq Studies, University College of Cape Breton Summer Institute at California Institute of Integral Studies.

Hoebel, E. Adamson. 1978. *The Cheyennes: Indians of the Great Plains.* Fort Worth, Texas: Harcourt Brace.

Humbatzmen. 1990. *Secrets of Mayan Science/Religion.* Santa Fe, MX: Bear and Co.

Jenness, Diamond. 1935. *Beings of the supernatural world. The Ojibwa Indians of Parry Island: Their Social and Religious Life.*

Anthropolgical Series # 17, Bulletin No. 78. Ottawa ON: Nat Mus of Canada.

Jiles, Paulette. 1995. *North Spirit.* Toronto ON: Doubleday Canada.

Johnson, Martha. 1992. Dene traditional Environmental Knowledge. *Akwekon J. 9* (2): 71-75.

Jones, Tom and Jones, Carolyn. 1995. *Maya Hieroglyphic Work Book.* Prepared for weekend workshops on Maya hieroglyphic writing. Arcata, California.

Kapiyo'ho, Lyons. 1997. Hawaiian Elder. Personal communication.

Knudston, Peter and Suzuki, David. 1992. *Wisdom of the Elders.* Toronto, ON: Stoddart.

Kremer, Jurgen. 1994. *Looking For Dame Yggdrasil.* Red Bluff, CA: Falkenflug Press.

Lyons, Oren. 1997. Elder and scholar born a Seneca and living as an Onondaga. Personal communication.

Mails, Thomas E. 1991. *Fools Crow: Wisdom and Power.* Tulsa, OK: Council Oaks Books.

Mills, Antonia. 1992. The meaningful universe: Intersecting forces in Beaver Indian cosmology. *In* David R. Miller, David R., Carl Beal, James Dempsey and R. Wesley Heber (Eds.), *First Ones: Readings in Indian/Native Studies.* pp. 226- 234. Piapot Reserve #75, Saskatchewan Indian Fed College.

Mills, Antonia. 1994. Reincarnation belief among North American Indians and Inuit: Context distribution, and variation. *In* Antonia Mills and Richard Slobodin (Eds.), *American Rebirth: Reincarnation Belief Among North American Indians and Inuit.* pp 15-37. Toronto, ON: University of Toronto Press.

Mills. Antonia. 1988. Reincarnation among the Beaver and Gitksan Indians. *Anthropologica 30*(1): 23 – 59.

Montour, Joel. 1993. Saving mother earth to save ourselves. *Parabala 18*(4):31-36.

Navaho Curriculum Center. 1971. *Navaho History.* Chinle, AZ: Rough Rock Demonstation School.

Niatum, Dianne. 1995. Tlinget family reunion. *Akwe-kon Jrnl 12*(1-2):48 – 52.

Ojibwa Cultural Foundation. 1990. Winnipeg, MB. Personal communication.

Ortiz, Alfonso. 1975. The Tewa world view. *In* Denis and Barbara Tedlock (Eds.), *Teachings From the American Earth: Indian Religion and Philosophy.* pp. 179-189. New York, NY: Liveright.

Peat, F. 1994. *Lighting the Seventh Fire:Spiritual Ways, Healing, and Science of Native Am.* NY: Carol Pub.

Peat, F. 1996. Indigenous Science. *Revision 12*:12 - 15.

Parker, Arthur C. 1989. *Seneca Myths & Folk Tales.* University of Nebraska Press: Bison Books.

Recinos, G. and M. 1950. *Popal Vuh: The Sacred Book of the Ancient Quiché Maya.* Norman,OK: Uof OK.

Roderico, Teni. 1989. Cosmological importance of corn among Mayan peoples. *Akwe:kon J. 7* (3):14-19.

Ross, A.C. 1989. *Mitakuye Oyasin: We are all related.* Denver, CO: Bear.

Smith, Theresa. 1991. Calling the Thunder, Part One: Animikeek, the thunderstorm as speech event in the Anishinaabe Life World. *American Indian Lecture and Research Journal 15*(3): 19-28.

Snake, Reuben. 1993. Living in Harmony with Nature. *Akwe-kon Journal, 10*(3):12-13.

Solomon, Arthur. 1994. *Eating Bitterness: A Vision Beyond Prison Walls.* Toronto, ON: NC Press.

Speck, Frank G. 1963. *Naskapi: The Savage Hunters of the Labrador Peninsula.* Norman, OK: U of OK.

Stiegelbauer, S.M. 1996. What is an Elder? What do Elders do? First Nations Elders as teachers in culture-based urban organizations. *Canadian J of Native Studies. 16*(1):37-66. Brandon, MB: U of B.

Toelken, Barre. 1976. *Seeing With a Native Eye: How Many Sheep Will It Hold.* NY, NY: Harper and Row.

Thomas, Jacob with Terry, Boyle. 1994. *Teachings From the Longhouse.* Toronto, ON: Stoddart.

Thomas, Jacob. 1997. Cayuga Elder and hereditary Chief of Iroquois Confederacy. Personal communication.

Tompkins, Peter. 1976. *Mysteries of the Mexican Pyramids.* London,UK: Thames and Hudson.

Velarde, Pablita. 1989. *Old Father Story Tellers.* Santa Fe, NM: Clear Light Publishers.

White, Tom. 1990. Planting time/Cherokee. *Parabola. 25*(1):18-20.

Williamson, Ray and Farrer, Clair. 1992. *Earth and Sky.* Albuquerque, NM: Univ of New Mexico Press.

About the Author

Dr. Brian Rice is of Mohawk/Finnish descent. He has taught in the departments of Native Studies at the University of Sudbury, International Development Studies at Menno Simmons College, and Continuing Education at University of Manitoba. Currently, Dr. Rice is a faculty member in the Department of Education at the University of Winnipeg in Manitoba, Canada.

Dr. Rice graduated with a Diploma in Aboriginal Education from McGill University, a Bachelor and Masters in Religious Studies from Concordia University; and a doctorate in Aboriginal Traditional Knowledge from the California Institute of Integral Studies.

Guidelines to Authors

Call for Papers

Aboriginal Issues Press produces one volume of refereed papers each year and welcomes scholarly papers relating to Aboriginal issues from all fields of study, including: traditional knowledge, social, physical and natural sciences, law, education, architecture, management, medicine, nursing, social work, physical education, engineering, environment, agriculture, art, music, drama, continuing education, and others. Aboriginal and non-Aboriginal authors from a wide range of backgrounds and from all geographic locations are welcome, including: scientists, poets, educators, elders, chiefs, students, and government personnel. All papers (ranging from scientific papers to poetry) are reviewed by scholars working in related fields.

Papers must be submitted in hard copy and on disk (Word) following the APA Writer's Style Manual 5th Edition. Maximum paper length is 10 pages, double spaced, 2.5 cm margins, 12 pt font, Times New Roman. Any photographs, charts, or graphs must be provided in digital format and are included in the 10 page count. Sources are included directly in the text; provide the author and date for paraphrased information, for example (Flett 1937, Graham 2001) and the author, date and page number for direct quotations, for example (Boas 1964, 33). Include full references to all sources in a section titled References at the end of the paper; for economy of space footnotes or endnotes will not be included. Capitalize Aboriginal Peoples, Native Peoples and First Nations. Convert all English measurements to metric. Include a 1-sentence biography, a 50 to 75 word abstract, and your return address with your submission. For further information please contact aboriginal-issues-press@umanitoba.ca

Books

Aboriginal Issues Press also publishes sole-authored books. Scholars interested in submitting a book manuscript for review must provide the following information to aboriginal-issues-press@umanitoba.ca

1. Table of contents;
2. Two sample chapters representative of the writing style;
3. A curriculum vitae of the author(s);
4. Samples of illustrations, photos, graphs, etc. for the publication;
5. A prospectus which includes the purpose, objectives, and how the author(s) acquired the knowledge shared in the manuscript;
6. A description of the audience and market; and
7. An explanation of why you chose *Aboriginal Issues Press* as a possible publisher.